Library Classification and

Numbering System

H. W. Parker

Alpha Editions

This edition published in 2020

ISBN : 9789354031748

Design and Setting By
Alpha Editions
email - alphaedis@gmail.com

LIBRARY CLASSIFICATION

AND

NUMBERING
SYSTEM

By

H. W. PARKER

Librarian

FREE LIBRARY OF
THE GENERAL SOCIETY OF MECHANICS AND TRADESMEN
of the City of New York

THIRD EDITION

NEW YORK CITY
1926

This book is not copyrighted, it is the outcome of the author's 51 years of practical library work, and whatever good is contained therein is freely given, so that the library may become more useful as a public institution.

First edition, 1901.
Second edition, 1910.
Third, enlarged edition, 1926.

Printed in the United States of America by
J. J. LITTLE AND IVES COMPANY, NEW YORK

INTRODUCTORY

This system is as nearly mnemonic as possible, intending to aid both the public and the library employees.

The classification system is arranged to fall in succession, each sub-class a relative part of the main class; it is divided into three parts—Class (A), sub-class (b), and a division (3).

Any person with an ordinary education and a small knowledge of books and their authors can find books, should the reader fail to supply either class letter or number, or both. Example: If a book on music is wanted the messenger will know that music is a fine art, Class F and a sub-class m (Music), where a guide card shows the numbered division wanted.

This system is more expansive than here represented, as not all the letters of the alphabet are used, leaving room for more classes, also a very few sub-classes or divisions are used up.

Books are classified: First, under subject; Second, by Author's numbered combination; Third, by initial letter or title of book. Example: Fiske, American Revolution; Hu.44059 a; Subject Hu. sub-class, 4: Fiske, 4059; initial letter of book, a; together making one shelf combination.

Biography is under the names of those written of, as Adams, Lincoln, Washington, sub-class, initial letter of the Author's name; Autobiography without sub-letter, see rule.

Use the correct name of an author and not the pseudonym, anonymous books are numbered under combination of the first word of title; Fiction alphabetically arranged under the title of book no letter or numbering used.

For the convenience of the public and to avoid confusion the sub-letters K and N are substituted for L and O, as both these letters where index cards are typewritten appear as extra numbers 1 and 0.

When there are several books with the same initial letter, as Da, Do, or in the case of biography where there are more than one of the same initial as: life of Washington, by Seelye, Sparks, Stoddard, the following scale is used as B,9479,s-2; B,9479,s-6; or B,9479,s-8.

Scale of sub-Numbers.

A to C —— 1	I to K —— 4	R to S —— 7
D to F —— 2	L to M —— 5	T to V —— 8
G to H —— 3	N to P —— 6	W to Z —— 9

CLASSIFICATION SYSTEM

CLASS A

AGRICULTURAL SCIENCE

A	AGRICULTURE—General Works.
A1	Exhibitions, Fairs, etc.
A2	Implements, Machinery.
A3	Domestic Animals, Dogs, Cats, etc.
A4	Dairy Farming, Grazing, Cattle, Sheep, Goats, Pigs.
A5	Dairy Farming, Butter, Cheese, Milk.
A6	Veterinary Science, Horse, Stable.
A7	Poultry, Pigeons.
A8	Bees, Silk-Worms.
A9	Country Life.
Af	FARMING—General Works.
Af1	Soils, Soildraining, Mucks, Fertilization.
Af2	Products of a Temperate Climate.
Af6	Tropical Products, Coffee, Tea, Cotton.
Af8	Pests.
Af9	Trees and Forestry.
Ag	GARDENING—General Works.
Ag1	Vegetables, Kitchen and Small Crops.
Ag3	Grape Culture, Fruits.
Ag4	Orchards.
Ag5	Floriculture, Window Gardening.
Ag6	Ornamental and Landscape Gardening.
Ag7	Hedges, Arbors.
Ag8	Ferns, Cactus and Rare Plants.
Ag9	Cemeteries, Catacombs.

CLASS B

BIOGRAPHY

B	BIOGRAPHY—Individual Under Names of the Persons Written of
Bc	BIOGRAPHY—Collective by Authors.

Bc1	Biographical Dictionaries and Annuals.
Bc2	Genealogy and Heraldry, General.
Bc3	Genealogy, United States.
Bc4	Genealogy, England.
Bo5	Genealogy, Germany.
Bc6	Genealogy, France, Spain, Italy.
Bc7	Genealogy, All other Countries than above.
Bc8	Names, Persons, Geographical.
Bc9	Flags.
Br	RELIGIOUS BIOGRAPHY—Individual.
Br1	Religious Biography, Collective.

CLASS C

COMMERCE, MILITARY AND NAVAL SCIENCE, NAVIGATION, SHIP AND YACHT BUILDING

C	COMMERCE—General Works.
C1	Shipping.
C2	Railroads, Express Companies, Transportation.
C4	Customs, Exportation.
C5	Post-office, Mails.
C6	Insurance, Life.
C7	Insurance, Fire.
C8	Insurance, Land, Marine.
C9	Insurance, Accident.
Cm	MILITARY SCIENCE—General Works, Academies.
Cm1	Military Science, Artillery, Gunnery, Ordnance, Strategy, Arms, Tactics.
Cm9	Military Architecture.
Cn	NAVAL SCIENCE—General Works, Academies.
Cn1	Naval Science, Life, Shells, Guns, Strategy, Tactics.
Cn5	Navigation, Seamanship.
Cn6	Life-saving Stations, Lighthouses.
Cn9	Naval Architecture.
Cs	SHIPBUILDING—General Works.
Cs1	Historical.
Cs2	Small Boats.
Cs3	Sailing Vessels.
Cs4	Yacht Building.
Cs5	Steamboats and Steamships.
Cs7	Motor Boats.
Cs9	Lighters, Barges, etc.

CLASS D

DOMESTIC ARTS

D   General Works, Household Management.
D1   Laundry Work.
D2   Dining.
D3   Cookery, Baking, Preserving.
D4   Coffee, Tea, etc.
D5   Confectionery.
D6   Chafing Dish.
D7   Condiments.
D8   Willow Work, Broom, Brush, and Basket Making.
D9   Furniture, Upholstery.
Db   BREWING, Liquors.
Db1 Wine, Vinegar.
Db2 Beers, Ales.
Db3 Artificial Waters.
Db9 Mixing of Drinks, etc.
Dc   CLOTHING and Other Domestic Arts.
Dc1 Dressmaking.
Dc2 Tailoring.
Dc3 Fancy Costumes.
Dc4 Millinery.
Dc5 Embroidery, Lace, Needlework.
Dc6 Beadwork.
Dc7 Artificial Flower, Paper Work.
Dc8 Toilet Articles, Perfumery.
Dc9 Pyroggraphy.

CLASS E

EDUCATION, BUSINESS, LANGUAGE, PHILOSOPHY

E   EDUCATION—General Works, Essays.
E1 Educational Systems, Schools, Colleges, Institutes, Universities.
E2 Female Education.
E3 Teaching.
E4 Special Studies.
E5 Self-Culture, Self Help, Success.
E6 Menticulture, Mnemonics.
E7 Etiquette, Social Forms.
E9 Literary Societies, Student Life.

Eb	BUSINESS—General Works, Historical.
Eb1	Efficiency—Management.
Eb2	Bookkeeping, Auditing, Accounting.
Eb3	Cost and Stock Keeping.
Eb4	Secretarial Work and Training, Writing, Correspondence.
Eb5	Shorthand, Stenography.
Eb6	Typewriting, Typewriter.
Eb7	Salesmanship, Purchasing.
Eb8	Advertising, Window Dressing.
Eb9	Catalogues, Furniture.
Ek	LANGUAGE—General Works.
Ek1	Philology.
Ek2	Composition, Rhetoric, Spelling, Writing.
Ek3	Use of Words, Conversation, Pronunciation.
Ek4	Grammars, English.
Ek5	Grammars, German, Norwegian, Swedish.
Ek6	Grammars, French.
Ek7	Grammars, Italian, Spanish, Portuguese.
Ek8	Grammars, Latin, Greek.
Ek9	Grammars, Oriental and other than above.
Ep	PHILOSOPHY—General Works.
Ep1	Philosophy, Ancient.
Ep2	Philosophy, Modern. Psychology.
Ep3	Logic, Reason, Knowledge.
Ep4	Emotions, Passions.
Ep5	Moral Philosophy, Ethics.
Ep6	Domestic Philosophy.
Ep7	Palmistry, Handwriting.
Ep8	Phrenology, Physiognomy.
Ep9	Occult Sciences, Astrology, Christian Science.

CLASS F

FINE ARTS

F	General Works.
F1	Æsthetics.
F2	Artists' Works and Biography, Individual.
F3	Artists' Works and Biography, Collective.
F4	Art Essays, Renaissance.
F5	Sacred and Legendary Art.
F6	Art Education.
F7	Art Societies.
F8	Galleries, Exhibitions, Catalogues.

F9	Historical.
Fa	ARCHITECTURE—General Works.
Fa1	Architecture, Roman, Gothic.
Fa2	Architecture, Church.
Fa3	Architecture, Civil, Schools, Theatres, Libraries.
Fa4	Architecture, Domestic.
Fa5	Architecture, Design and Construction.
Fa6	Furniture and Cabinet Making.
Fa7	Architectural Societies.
Fa8	Decoration, House Beautiful.
Fa9	Historical.
Fc	CERAMICS.
Fc1	China and Pottery Painting.
Fc2	Stained Glass.
Fd	DRAWING and PAINTING—General Works.
Fd1	Drawing and Painting, Practical, Portraits, Sketching.
Fd2	Drawing and Painting, Freehand, Illustration.
Fd3	Drawing, Mechanical, Architectural, Geometrical.
Fd4	Drawing, Decorative.
Fd5	Drawing, Anatomical.
Fd6	Crafts and Art, Metal Work.
Fd7	Sculpture, Bronzes, Tablets, Monuments.
Fd8	Book Arts, Printing, Stereotyping.
Fd9	Lettering, Alphabets, Monograms.
Fe	ENGRAVING—General Works, Prints, Etc.
Fe1	Engraving Designs.
Fe3	Engraving, Dies, Seals.
Fe5	Engraving, Coins, Medals.
Fe6	Engraving, Postage, Stamps.
Fe7	Gems and Precious Stones.
Fe8	Jewelry.
Fe9	Historical, Hall-marks.
Fm	MUSIC—General Works.
Fm1	Composition, Technique, Conducting.
Fm2	Instruction Books.
Fm3	Vocal Music.
Fm4	Instrumental Music.
Fm5	Sacred Music.
Fm6	Books on Opera, Oratorio, Cantatas.
Fm7	Voice, Art of Singing.
Fm8	Construction and use of Musical Instruments.
Fm9	Musical History, Dictionaries.
Fp	PHOTOGRAPHY—General Works.
Fp1	Collections.

Fp2	Supplies, Cameras.
Fp3	Photographic Chemistry.
Fp4	Special Processes.
Fp5	Special Uses of Photography, Animals, Buildings, Surveying, etc.
Fp7	Photo-lithography, Zincography.
Fp8	Photo-engraving and Electrographing.
Fp9	Photo-micography.
Fs	SPORTS—General Works, Pastimes.
Fs1	ATHLETICS.
Fs2	AMUSEMENTS—Public.
Fs3	Amusements, Parlor Billiards, Cards.
Fs4	ENTERTAINMENT—Indoors, Dancing, Puzzles.
Fs5	Conjuring, Ventriloquism.
Fs6	Boating, Yacht Racing.
Fs7	Fishing, Swimming.
Fs8	Archery, Bicycling, Tennis, Skating, Polo, Horsemanship.
Fs9	Hunting, Trapping, Mountaineering.

CLASS G

GENERAL WORKS

G	General and Unclassified Works.
G1	Book Seller's Catalogues.
G2	Bibliography, Pseudonyms.
G3	Library Management.
G4	Library Economy.
G5	Library Catalogues, Public.
G6	Library Catalogues, Private.
G8	Prohibited Books.
G9	Old Books, First Editions.
GM	MAGAZINES—General.
Gm1	Magazines, Literary.
Gm2	Magazines, Scientific.
Gm3	Magazines, Medical.
Gm4	Magazines, Religious.
Gm5	NEWSPAPERS—Daily.
Gm6	Newspapers—Weekly.
Gm7	PERIODICALS—General.
Gm8	Periodicals, Scientific, Medical.
Gm9	Periodicals, All others.
Gp	PAMPHLETS—General.
Gp1	Pamphlets, Biographical.

Gp2	Pamphlets, Educational, Literary.
Gp3	Pamphlets, Historical.
Gp4	Pamphlets, Medical.
Gp5	Pamphlets, Political, Social.
Gp6	Pamphlets, Religious.
Gp7	Pamphlets, Scientific.
Gp8	Pamphlets, Useful and Fine Arts.
Gp9	Pamphlets, Voyages and Travels.
Gr	REFERENCE Books, Directories Under Cities.
Gr1	Annuals, Year Books.
Gr2	Encyclopædias.
Gr3	Dictionaries, English.
Gr4	Dictionaries, German.
Gr5	Dictionaries, French.
Gr6	Dictionaries, Spanish, Italian, Portuguese.
Gr7	Dictionaries, Latin.
Gr8	Dictionaries, Greek.
Gr9	Dictionaries, All other Languages than above.

CLASS H

HISTORY

H	HISTORY—General Works.
H1	History, Essays.
H2	History, Ancient.
H3	History, Modern.
H4	History, Universal.
H5	Classical Dictionaries.
H6	Chronology, Handbooks.
H7	Civilization.
H8	Manners and Customs.
H9	Secret Societies.
Ha	AMERICA—General Works.
Ha1	Iceland, Greenland, Labrador.
Ha2	British America, Nova Scotia, Canada.
Ha3	Alaska.
Ha4	Central America.
Ha5	Mexico.
Ha6	West Indies, Bermuda, Martinique.
Ha7	Porto Rico, Cuba.
Ha8	South America.
Hb	BRITISH History—General Works.
Hb1	British History, England, Separate Cities and Towns.

Hb2	British History, Ireland, General Works.
Hb3	British History, Ireland, Separate Cities and Towns.
Hb4	British History, Scotland, Wales, Isle of Man.
Hb5	British History, Scotland, Separate Cities and Towns.
Hb7	British History, Army and Navy.
Hc	CHINA—Korea, Tibet, Manchuria.
Hc1	JAPAN.
Hc2	OCEANICA—Hawaii, Philippines.
Hc3	AUSTRALIA—Malaysia.
Hc4	SIAM—Anam, Burmah.
Hc5	INDIA—Afghanistan, Beluchistan.
Hc6	PERSIA—Parthenia.
Hc7	TURKEY in Asia—Palestine.
Hc8	JEWS.
Hc9	ASIA—General Works.
Hd	DENMARK—General Works.
Hd1	Denmark, Separate Cities and Towns.
Hd2	Denmark, Army and Navy.
Hd3	NORWAY—General Works.
Hd4	Norway, Separate Cities and Towns.
Hd5	Norway, Army and Navy.
Hd6	SWEDEN—General Works.
Hd7	Sweden, Separate Cities and Towns.
Hd8	Sweden, Army and Navy.
Hd9	Lapland.
He	EGYPT—Nile, Nubia.
He1	Egypt, Separate Places.
Hf	FRANCE—General Works.
Hf1	France, Separate Cities and Towns.
Hf6	France, Alsace Lorraine.
Hf7	France, Army and Navy.
Hf8	SWITZERLAND—General Works.
Hf9	Switzerland, Separate Cities and Towns.
Hg	GERMANY—General Works.
Hg1	Germany, Separate Cities and Towns.
Hg2	Germany, Army and Navy.
Hg3	AUSTRIA—Hungary.
Hg4	Bohemia, Bosnia, Czechoslovakia, Roumania, Tyrol.
Hg5	Bavaria.
Hg6	Bulgaria, Servia, Montenegro.
Hg8	Belgium.
Hg9	HOLLAND—Netherlands.
Hi	ITALY—General Works.
Hi1	Italy, Separate Cities and Towns.

Hi2	Corsica, Malta, Sicily, Sardinia.
Hi7	Italy, Army and Navy.
Hk	ROME, Ancient.
Hk5	GREECE—Cyprus.
Hn	NORTH POLE.
Hn1	Arctic Regions.
Hn2	Antarctic Regions.
Ho	TURKEY.
Ho1	Turkey, Separate Places.
Ho2	AFRICA—General Works.
Ho3	Africa—Northern Algeria, British Somaliland, Carthage, French Africa, Sahara, Tunis.
Ho4	Africa—Eastern, Abyssinia, British East Africa, German East Africa, Italian Somaliland, Mozambique, Portuguese East Africa, Somaliland.
Ho5	Africa—Central, Angola, Belgium, Congo, Congo Free States, Nigeria, Nyasaland, Uganda, Zanzibar.
Ho6	Africa—Western, Dahomey, Gambia, Gold Coast, Guinea, Kamerun, Liberia, Sierra Leone, Togoland.
Ho7	Africa—Southern, Bechuanaland, Cape Colony, Damaraland, Kaffraria, Natal, Rhodesia, South African Republic, Swaziland, Transvaal.
Ho8	Madagascar, Mauritius, Morocco, Orange Free State.
Hr	RUSSIA—General Works, Crimea.
Hr1	Russia, Separate Cities and Towns.
Hr2	Russia, Siberia, Poland, Finland.
Hr7	Russia, Army and Navy.
Hs	SPAIN—General Works.
Hs1	Spain, Separate Cities and Towns.
Hs3	Spain, Army and Navy.
Hs4	PORTUGAL—General Works.
Hs5	Portugal, Separate Cities and Towns.
Hs6	Portugal, Army and Navy.
Hs7	Balearic Islands, Madeira.
Hu	UNITED STATES of AMERICA—Descriptive Works.
Hu1	United States of America, Indians.
Hu2	United States of America, Colonial History.
Hu3	United States of America, General History.
Hu4	United States of America, History 1775–1800.
Hu5	United States of America, History 1801–1859.
Hu6	United States of America, History 1860–1865.
Hu7	United States of America, History 1866–1900.
Hu8	United States of America, History 1901–
Hu9	United States of America, Separate States, Cities, towns, etc.

JURISPRUDENCE, LAW

J	General and Historical Works.
Ja	Ancient, Feudal, Canon Law.
Jc	Constitutional Law.
Jm	Martial Law.
Jn	National, International Law.
Jp	Practical, Domestic Law.
Jr	Rules of Debate, Parliamentary Law.
Js	Special Law.
Jt	Trials, Courts, Criminal Law.

CLASS L

LITERATURE

L	General Works.
L1	Literary Collections.
L2	Works of Individual Authors.
L3	Literature, General Works.
L4	Literature, English, American.
L5	Literature, French, Spanish, Italian, Portuguese.
L6	Literature, German, Norwegian, Swedish.
L7	Literature, Greek, Latin.
L8	Literature, Oriental.
L9	Literature, Others than above.
Lb	BOOKS—What to Read.
Lb1	Authorship.
Lb2	Journalism.
Lb3	Literary Criticism.
Lb4	Literary Curiosities.
Lb8	Anagrams, Anecdotes, Fables.
Lb9	Book-Plates.
Le	ESSAYS—General Works.
Le1	Essays, English, American.
Le4	Essays, French, Italian.
Le5	Essays, Spanish, Portuguese.
Le6	Essays, German.
Le7	Essays, Greek and Latin.
Le8	Essays, Indian, Persian.
Le9	Essays, Other than above.
Lo	ORATORY—Debating, Elocution, Gesture.
Lo5	Speeches, Addresses, Individual.

Lo6	Speeches, Addresses, Collections
Lp	POETRY—General Works, English, American, Criticism.
Lp1	DRAMA—General Works, English, American, Criticism.
Lp2	Poetry, Plays, English, American, Individual Authors.
Lp3	Poetry, Plays, English, American, Collections.
Lp4	Poetry, Juvenile, Amateur Theatricals.
Lp5	Poetry, French, Spanish, Portuguese.
Lp6	Poetry, German.
Lp7	Poetry, Greek and Latin.
Lp8	Poetry, Indian, Persian.
Lp9	Poetry, other than above.
Lq	QUOTATION, Proverbs, Maxims.
Lr	READERS—Speakers.
Ls	SHAKESPEARE—Collected Works.
Ls1	Shakespeare, Separate Plays.
Ls2	Shakespeare, Criticism.
Ls3	Shakespeare, Life under Writer or Editor.
Ls4	Bacon Controversy.
Ls9	Theatres, Playhouses Devoted to Shakespeare.
Lw	WIT and HUMOR—General Works.
Lw1	Wit and Humor to end of 15th Century.
Lw2	Wit and Humor—16th Century.
Lw3	Wit and Humor—17th Century.
Lw4	Wit and Humor—18th Century.
Lw5	Wit and Humor—19th Century.
Lw6	Wit and Humor—20th Century.
Lw7	Drawings.
Lw8	Comic Pictures.
Lw9	Comic Pictures, Animals.

CLASS M

MEDICAL SCIENCE

M	General and Unclassified Medical Books and Essays.
M1	Pharmacy, Annuals and Dictionaries.
M2	Bacteriology.
M3	Theory and Practice of Medicine, Diseases.
M4	Skin Diseases.
M5	Nervous System, Brain and Spine.
M6	Insanity, Degeneration and Suicide.
M7	Temperance and Intemperance, Poisons, Narcotics, Stimulants.
M8	Domestic Medicines, Nursing, Aids to the Injured, Hospitals.
M9	Massage, Hydropathy, Health Resorts.

Ma	ANATOMY AND PHYSIOLOGY—General Works.
Ma1	Anatomy.
Ma2	Physiology.
Mb	BIOLOGY AND EVOLUTION—General Works.
Mb2	Darwinism.
Mb3	Heredity.
Me	DISEASES OF THE EYE, EAR, ETC.—General Works.
Me1	Ear.
Me2	Eye.
Me4	Nose.
Me5	Throat and Lung Disease.
Mf	FOOD, DIET, ETC.—General Works.
Mf1	Food, Digestion, Nutrition and Adulteration.
Mf2	Disorders of the Stomach and Treatment.
Mf9	Privation, Starvation, Fasting, Luxury.
Mg	GENERATION, GYNECOLOGY, ETC.—General Works.
Mg1	Gynecology.
Mg2	Obstetrics.
Mg3	Advice to Women.
Mg4	Children's Diseases and Care.
Mg5	Sexual Science, General Works.
Mg6	Sexual Science, Special Subjects.
Mg8	Advice to Men.
Mg9	Sexual Science, Diseases and Treatment.
Mh	HYGIENE—General Works.
Mh1	Public Hygiene, Sanitary Science.
Mh2	Longevity, Old Age.
Mh3	Beauty, Art of.
Mh4	Baths and Bathing.
Mh5	Sleep, Rest, Fatigue.
Mh6	Head, Hair.
Mh7	Hands.
Mh8	Feet.
Mh9	Hygienic Measures, Burial, Embalming, Cremation.
Mp	PHYSICAL EDUCATION.
Mp1	Delsarte, Vocal Elocution.
Ms	Surgery—General Works.
Ms6	Surgical Appliances.
Ms7	Dentistry.

CLASS N

NATURAL HISTORY

N	ANTHROPOLOGY, Creation, Antiquity.
N2	Races of Men.
Na	ASTRONOMY.
Na1	Sun, Moon, Stars.
Na2	Planets, Comets, Meteors.
Na3	Earth.
Na4	Planetary Effect on Water.
Na5	Telescopes and other Astronomical Instruments.
Na6	Maps.
Na7	Geodesy.
Na8	Astronomical Surveying.
Na9	Chronology, Horology, Time.
Ng	GEOLOGY—General Works.
Ng1	Earth's Surface.
Ng2	Glacial Period.
Ng3	Paleontology.
Ng4	Man.
Ng5	Plants, Animals.
Ng6	Mineralogy.
Ng7	Meteorology.
Ng8	Physical Geography.
Ng9	Hydrology.
Nh	NATURAL HISTORY—General Works.
Nh1	Botany.
Nh2	Ferns, Trees, Grasses.
Nh3	Zoology.
Nh4	Insects.
Nh5	Microscope, Taxidermy.
Nh6	Marine Zoology, Reptiles.
Nh7	Birds.
Nh8	Mammals.
Nh9	Nature Study, Animal Stories.

CLASS P

PHYSICS, MATHEMATICS

P	PHYSICS—General Works.
P1	Natural Philosophy.
P2	Chromatics, Light, Optics, Telescope.

P3	Force, Heat, Pyrometry.
P4	Acoustics, Sound.
P5	Pneumatics, Gas, Air.
P6	Energy.
P8	Liquids, Hydraulics.
P9	Aeronautics.
Pc	CHEMISTRY—General Works.
Pc1	Cyclopedias, Alchemy.
Pc2	Qualitative, Spectrum.
Pc3	Quantitative.
Pc4	Laboratory.
Pc5	Inorganic.
Pc6	Organic.
Pc7	Physiological.
Pc9	Technology, Manufactures.
Pe	ELECTRICITY—General Works.
Pe1	Magnetism.
Pe2	Electric Current, Battery.
Pe3	Electric Engineering.
Pe4	Dynamo, Motor, Machinery.
Pe5	Railways.
Pe6	Light, Heat.
Pe7	Bells, Wiring.
Pe8	Telephone, Telegraph.
Pe9	Unusual Subjects or Applications.
Pm	MATHEMATICS—General Works.
Pm1	Arithmetic.
Pm2	Interest Tables.
Pm3	Algebra, Calculus, Logarithms.
Pm4	Geometry, Conic Sections.
Pm5	Metric System, Weights and Measures.
Pm6	Surveying, Trigonometry.
Pm8	Probabilities, Exchange.
Pm9	Special Subjects—Drawing, Engineering, Statistics.

CLASS R

REPORTS, PUBLIC DOCUMENTS

R	General Works.
R1	Agricultural.
R2	Architectural.
R3	Charities, Health.
R4	Educational.

R5	Medical.
R6	Labor.
R7	Law.
R8	Political, Social.
R9	Scientific, Technological.
*Rn	NEW YORK STATE, Assembly, Senate.
Rn1	Agriculture.
Rn2	Education.
Rn3	Fish and Game.
Rn4	Health.
Rn5	Labor.
Rn6	Charities.
Rn7	Separate Places in New York State under Place.
Rn8	New York County, Under Departments.
Rn9	New York City, Under Departments.
Ru	UNITED STATES—Messages and Documents of the Presidents.
Ru1	Agriculture, Post Office.
Ru2	Attorney-General.
Ru3	House of Representatives.
Ru4	Interior.
Ru5	Navy.
Ru6	Senate.
Ru7	State.
Ru8	Treasury.
Ru9	War.

* For other Cities or States, substitute initial letter after 'R' as above.

CLASS S

SOCIAL AND POLITICAL SCIENCE

S	SOCIAL SCIENCE—General Works.
S1	Periodicals, Magazines.
S2	Statistics.
S3	Crime, Prisons, Secret Service, Reformatories.
S4	Charities, Poverty, State.
S5	Church and Sociology.
S6	Slavery, Negro.
S7	Woman, Domestic Conditions.
S8	Woman, Employment, Suffrage.
S9	Social Settlements, Charitable Associations.
Se	ECONOMY—General Works, Free Trade, Protection.
Se1	Progress, Trusts, Unions, Guilds.

Se2	Land, Rents, Ownership.
Se3	Immigration, Colonization, Population.
Se4	Capital, Wages, Labor.
Se5	Communism, Socialism.
Se6	Convict Labor, Contracts.
Se7	Finance, State, National.
Se8	Banks and Banking.
Se9	Building, Loan Companies, **Pawnbroking.**
Sg	GOVERNMENTS—State, City.
Sg1	Finance.
Sg2	Building.
Sg3	License.
Sg4	Engineering.
Sg5	Health, Charities.
Sg6	Public Works.
Sg7	Parks, Lighting.
Sg8	Police, Detectives.
Sg9	Fire.
Sp	POLITICAL—General Works.
Sp1	Forms.
Sp2	Parties.
Sp3	United States.
Sp4	Great Britain.
Sp5	France, Switzerland.
Sp6	Germany, Holland, Austria.
Sp7	Spain, Portugal, Italy, Russia.
Sp8	Sweden, Denmark, Norway.
Sp9	Other Countries than above.

CLASS T

THEOLOGY, RELIGION

T	THEOLOGY—General Works, Philosophy, Theories.
T1	Seminaries.
T2	Bible, Special Books, Bible Studies.
T3	Bible Commentaries, Apocryphal, Exegetical Works.
T4	Doctrinal and Dogmatic Theology.
T5	Christology, Trinity.
T6	Heaven, Hell, Salvation.
T7	Homiletics, Sermons, Pastoral, Theology.
T8	Church Sacraments, Ceremonies, Church **Furnishings. Vest**ments, Hymnology.
T9	Devotional and Practical Theology.

Tc	CHRISTIAN RELIGION—General Works, Reformation, Inquisition.
Tc1	Natural Theology, Agnosticism, Deism, Atheism, Infidelity, Heresies.
Tc2	Roman Catholic, Greek, Oriental.
Tc3	Protestant Episcopal.
Tc4	Baptist, Methodist, Wesleyans, General Protestant Sects.
Tc5	Presbyterian.
Tc6	Congregational, Reformed, Lutheran, Unitarian.
Tc7	Adventist, Swedenborgian.
Tc8	Mystics, Quakers, Mennonites, Etc.
Tc9	Parochial, Ragged and Sunday Schools, Revivals, Evangelistic, Mission.
Tn	NON-CHRISTIAN—General Works.
Tn1	Brahmanism, Buddism.
Tn2	Judaism.
Tn3	Mohammedanism.
Tn4	Others than above.
Tn5	Mythology, General Work.
Tn6	Mythology, Greek, Roman.
Tn7	Mythology, Norse, Teutonic.
Tn8	Mythology, Russian, Oriental, Barbarous.
Tn9	Mythology, American, Great Britain.

CLASS U

USEFUL ARTS

U	USEFUL ARTS—General Works, Exhibition, Fairs.
U1	Dictionaries, Cyclopedias.
U2	Receipts.
U3	Patents, Inventions.
Ub	BUILDING—General Works, Estimates, Plans.
Ub1	Building, Bricks, Stone, Masonry.
Ub2	Building, Cement, Mortar.
Ub3	CARPENTRY—General Works, Tools.
Ub4	Carpentry, Fitting, Joinery, Stair Work, Woodwork.
Ub5	Roofing.
Ub6	Painting, Graining, Varnishing.
Ub7	Paper Hanging.
Ub8	Plumbing, Gas Fitting.
Ub9	Heating, Ventilation, Sanitation.
Ue	ENGINEERING—General Works.
Ue1	Engineering, Mechanical Power.

Ue2	Engineering, Foundry Work.
Ue3	Engineering, Machinery (Complete).
Ue4	Engineering, Marine.
Ue5	Engineering, Steam Engine, Locomotive.
Ue6	Engineering, Civil, Strength of Materials.
Ue7	Engineering, Railroad Construction, Equipment, Management.
Ue8	Engineering, Hydraulic.
Ue9	Engineering, Mining, Metallurgy.
Uf	FUELS—General Works.
Uf1	Gas Manufacturing, Lighting.
Uf2	Fire.
Um	MANUFACTURES—General Works, Wood.
Um1	Iron, Steel, Tin.
Um2	Brass, Bronze, Copper.
Um3	Paper, Hair.
Um4	Glass, Earthenware.
Um5	Rubber, Glue, Gum, Flour, Starch.
Um6	Paints, Pigments.
Um7	Blacking, Candles, Ink, Soap.
Um8	Linen, Silk, Wool, Cotton.
Um9	Bleaching, Cleaning, Dyeing.
Ut	TRADES—General Works.
Ut1	Carriage, Wagon.
Ut2	Guns, Locks, Pistols.
Ut3	Clock, Watch, Instruments.
Ut4	Blacksmithing, Horseshoeing.
Ut5	Automobile.
Ut6	Harness, Leather, Shoes.
Ut7	Book-binding, Box-making.
Ut8	Hats, Caps, Gloves.
Ut9	Trunks, Umbrellas, Etc.

CLASS V

VOYAGES, TRAVELS

V	VOYAGES—General Works.
V1	Atlases, Georgraphies, Gazetteers.
V2	Guide Books, General.
V3	Voyages.
V4	Voyages of Discovery.
V5	Whale Fishing.
V6	Buccaneers, Pirates.
V7	Life and Adventures at Sea.

V8	TRAVELS—General Works.
V9	Travel Stories.
Va	AMERICA—General Works, Guide Books.
Va1	America, North.
Va2	America, British.
Va4	America, Central.
Va5	Mexico.
Va6	America, West Indies, Cuba, Bermuda, Porto Rico.
Va8	America, South.
Vb	BRITISH—General Works, Guide Books.
Vb1	British, England.
Vb2	British, Ireland.
Vb3	British, Scotland, Wales.
Vo	CHINA.
Vc1	JAPAN.
Vc2	OCEANICA.
Vc3	AUSTRALIA.
Vc4	SIAM, etc.
Vc5	INDIA, Afghanistan.
Vc6	PERSIA, etc.
Vc7	HOLY LAND, BABYLON.
Vc9	ASIA, General Works.
Vd	DENMARK—NORWAY, SWEDEN, LAPLAND.
Ve	EGYPT.
Vf	FRANCE.
Vf8	SWITZERLAND.
Vg	GERMANY.
Vg3	AUSTRIA.
Vg5	BAVARIA.
Vg8	BELGIUM.
Vg9	HOLLAND, Netherlands.
Vi	ITALY.
Vk	ROME, Ancient.
Vk5	GREECE.
Vm	MEDITERRANEAN Travels.
Vn	NORTH POLE.
Vn1	ARCTIC REGIONS.
Vn2	ANTARCTIC REGIONS.
Vo	TURKEY.
Vo2	AFRICA—General Works.
Vo3	Africa, North.
Vo4	Africa, East.
Vo5	Africa, Central.
Vo6	Africa, West.

Vo7   Africa, South.
Vr   RUSSIA.
Vs   SPAIN.
Vu   UNITED STATES.

NUMBERING SYSTEM

—A—

A	1001	Ackerm	1036
Aarons	1002	Ackerson	1037
Ab	1003	Ackert	1038
Abb	1004	Acr	1039
Abbe	1005	Acrn	1040
Abbey	1006	Act	1041
Abbot	1007	Acu	1042
Abbott	1008	Ad	1043
Abc	1009	Adami	1044
Abd	1010	Adams	1045
Abe	1011	Adamson	1046
Abel	1012	Add	1047
Abele	1013	Addi	1048
Abeli	1014	Addison	1049
Abelo	1015	Addo	1050
Aber	1016	Ade	1051
Aberl	1017	Adel	1052
Abi	1018	Adem	1053
Abl	1019	Adg	1054
Abm	1020	Adi	1055
Abo	1021	Adj	1056
Abr	1022	Adl	1057
Abrahams	1023	Adll	1058
Abram	1024	Adm	1059
Abrams	1025	Ado	1060
Abre	1026	Adr	1061
Abro	1027	Ads	1062
Abt	1028	Ae	1063
Ac	1029	Aes	1064
Ace	1030	Af	1065
Ach	1031	Afr	1066
Achn	1032	Ag	1067
Ack	1033	Age	1068
Acker	1034	Agn	1069
Ackerl	1035	Ago	1070

Agr	1071	Ald	1114
Agu	1072	Alden	1115
Ah	1073	Alder	1116
Aher	1074	Aldr	1117
Ahl	1075	Ale	1118
Ahle	1076	Ales	1119
Ahlo	1077	Alex	1120
Ahm	1078	Alf	1121
Ahn	1079	Alfi	1122
Ahr	1080	Alfo	1123
Ahrens	1081	Alfr	1124
Ahs	1082	Alg	1125
Ai	1083	Alh	1126
Aie	1084	Ali	1127
Aik	1085	All	1128
Aiki	1086	Allan	1129
Aikm	1087	Allar	1130
Aim	1088	Allb	1131
Ain	1089	Allc	1132
Ainsworth	1090	Alld	1133
Air	1091	Alle	1134
Ais	1092	Allen	1135
Ait	1093	Aller	1136
Aj	1094	Alles	1137
Ak	1095	Alley	1138
Ake	1096	Allg	1139
Aki	1097	Alli	1140
Akr	1098	Allig	1141
Al	1099	Allin	1142
Alam	1100	Allis	1143
Alb	1101	Allm	1144
Albany	1102	Alls	1145
Albe	1103	Allu	1146
Albert	1104	Alm	1147
Alberti	1105	Almi	1148
Albi	1106	Almo	1149
Albo	1107	Almy	1150
Albr	1108	Aln	1151
Albri	1109	Alo	1152
Albro	1110	Alp	1153
Albu	1111	Alpi	1154
Alc	1112	Alps	1155
Alco	1113	Als	1156

A—Continued.

Also	1157	Andres	1200
Alt	1158	Andrew	1201
Alte	1159	Andri	1202
Alter	1160	Andro	1203
Alth	1161	Andeu	1204
Althe	1162	Ang	1205
Altho	1163	Angell	1206
Alti	1164	Anger	1207
Altm	1165	Angi	1208
Alto	1166	Ango	1209
Alts	1167	Angs	1210
Alu	1168	Anh	1211
Alv	1169	Ani	1212
Alvi	1170	Ank	1213
Alvo	1171	Ann	1214
Am	1172	Anni	1215
Aman	1173	Annu	1216
Amb	1174	Ans	1217
Ambl	1175	Anse	1218
Ambr	1176	Anso	1219
Ambro	1177	Anst	1220
Amd	1178	Ant	1221
Ame	1179	Anth	1222
Amer	1180	Anthony	1223
American	1181	Anti	1224
Amerm	1182	Anto	1225
Ames	1183	Antr	1226
Ami	1184	Anz	1227
Aml	1185	Ap	1228
Amm	1186	Apf	1229
Amo	1187	Apg	1230
Amr	1188	Api	1231
Ams	1189	Apo	1232
Amso	1190	App	1233
Amt	1191	Appell	1234
An	1192	Appen	1235
Anc	1193	Apple	1236
And	1194	Appleb	1237
Anderson	1195	Appleg	1238
Anderton	1196	Appleton	1239
Andes	1197	Appley	1240
Andr	1198	Appr	1241
Andre	1199	Apt	1242

23

Baer	1406	Balt	1449
Baes	1407	Balti	1450
Baet	1408	Baltu	1451
Baf	1409	Balz	1452
Bag	1410	Bam	1453
Bagg	1411	Bamb	1454
Bagge	1412	Bambi	1455
Baggo	1413	Bame	1456
Bagl	1414	Ban	1457
Bagn	1415	Banc	1458
Bah	1416	Band	1459
Bahn	1417	Bandl	1460
Bahr	1418	Bane	1461
Bai	1419	Banf	1462
Bail	1420	Bang	1463
Bailey	1421	Bangs	1464
Baili	1422	Banh	1465
Bailw	1423	Bank	1466
Bain	1424	Banks	1467
Bair	1425	Bann	1468
Bais	1426	Banne	1469
Baj	1427	Banni	1470
Baker	1428	Banno	1471
Bakew	1429	Bans	1472
Bal	1430	Banta	1473
Bald	1431	Banto	1474
Baldw	1432	Banz	1475
Bale	1433	Bap	1476
Bales	1434	Bar	1477
Balf	1435	Barb	1478
Bali	1436	Barbe	1479
Balk	1437	Barbi	1480
Ball	1438	Barbo	1481
Balla	1439	Barc	1482
Balle	1440	Bard	1483
Balli	1441	Barde	1484
Ballis	1442	Bardes	1485
Ballm	1443	Bardi	1486
Ballo	1444	Bardo	1487
Ballu	1445	Bardu	1488
Balm	1446	Bare	1489
Balo	1447	Barg	1490
Bals	1448	Barh	1491

Bari	1492	Bartl	1535
Bario	1493	Bartley	1536
Bark	1494	Bartm	1537
Barke	1495	Barto	1538
Barkl	1496	Barton	1539
Barkle	1497	Bartow	1540
Barkli	1498	Barts	1541
Barl	1499	Baru	1542
Barli	1500	Barw	1543
Barlo	1501	Bas	1544
Barm	1502	Base	1545
Barn	1503	Bash	1546
Barnard	1504	Basi	1547
Barnd	1505	Bask	1548
Barnes	1506	Basl	1549
Barnet	1507	Bass	1550
Barnett	1508	Basse	1551
Barnew	1509	Basset	1552
Barney	1510	Bassf	1553
Barnf	1511	Basso	1554
Barno	1512	Bast	1555
Barnu	1513	Basti	1556
Baro	1514	Bat	1557
Barone	1515	Batchelor	1558
Barr	1516	Bate	1559
Barre	1517	Bates	1560
Barret	1518	Bath	1561
Barri	1519	Bati	1562
Barrin	1520	Bato	1563
Barrio	1521	Bats	1564
Barro	1522	Batt	1565
Barrow	1523	Batte	1566
Barry	1524	Batti	1567
Bars	1525	Battle	1568
Barst	1526	Batto	1569
Bart	1527	Bau	1570
Bartel	1528	Baud	1571
Barten	1529	Bauer	1572
Barter	1530	Baugh	1573
Barth	1531	Baum	1574
Barthe	1532	Bauma	1575
Bartho	1533	Baumann	1576
Barti	1534	Baume	1577

Bei	1664	Bendl	1707
Beie	1665	Bene	1708
Beil	1666	Benedict	1709
Beim	1667	Benedick	1710
Bein	1668	Benef	1711
Beir	1669	Benes	1712
Beis	1670	Benf	1713
Beiss	1671	Beng	1714
Beit	1672	Benh	1715
Bej	1673	Benj	1716
Bek	1674	Benk	1717
Bel	1675	Benl	1718
Beld	1676	Benn	1719
Beldi	1677	Benne	1720
Bele	1678	Bennet	1721
Belf	1679	Bennett	1722
Belg	1680	Benni	1723
Beli	1681	Benno	1724
Belk	1682	Beno	1725
Bell	1683	Bens	1726
Bella	1684	Benson	1727
Bellb	1685	Bent	1728
Belle	1686	Bente	1729
Bellet	1687	Bentl	1730
Bellew	1688	Benton	1731
Belli	1689	Benz	1732
Bellm	1690	Benzo	1733
Bello	1691	Beo	1734
Bellow	1692	Ber	1735
Belm	1693	Berb	1736
Belo	1694	Berc	1737
Bels	1695	Berd	1738
Belt	1696	Bere	1739
Belv	1697	Berf	1740
Belz	1698	Berg	1741
Bem	1699	Berge	1742
Bemi	1700	Bergen	1743
Ben	1701	Berger	1744
Benc	1702	Berges	1745
Bend	1703	Bergh	1746
Bender	1704	Bergi	1747
Bendh	1705	Bergl	1748
Bendi	1706	Bergm	1749

Bergmann	1750	Bert	1793
Bergn	1751	Berti	1794
Bergo	1752	Berto	1795
Bergs	1753	Bertr	1796
Berh	1754	Berts	1797
Beri	1755	Berw	1798
Berj	1756	Bes	1799
Berk	1757	Bese	1800
Berkm	1758	Besi	1801
Berko	1759	Beso	1802
Berkow	1760	Bess	1803
Berks	1761	Bessi	1804
Berl	1762	Besso	1805
Berle	1763	Best	1806
Berli	1764	Bet	1807
Berlini	1765	Beti	1808
Berlo	1766	Bett	1809
Berls	1767	Betti	1810
Berman	1768	Betts	1811
Bermann	1769	Betz	1812
Bermi	1770	Beu	1813
Bermn	1771	Beus	1814
Bern	1772	Bev	1815
Bernardi	7173	Bevi	1816
Bernb	1774	Beyer	1817
Bernd	1775	Beyerd	1818
Berne	1776	Beyh	1819
Bernes	1777	Bez	1820
Bernf	1778	Bia	1821
Bernhard	1779	Bian	1822
Bernhardt	1780	Biar	1823
Bernhe	1781	Bib	1824
Bernho	1782	Bible	1825
Berni	1783	Bic	1826
Berno	1784	Bick	1827
Berns	1785	Bicke	1828
Bero	1786	Bickl	1829
Berr	1787	Bickm	1830
Berri	1788	Bickn	1831
Berrie	1789	Bico	1832
Berry	1790	Bid	1833
Berrym	1791	Bido	1834
Bers	1792	Bie	1835

Bied	1836	Birn	1879
Bieh	1837	Birr	1880
Biel	1838	Bis	1881
Biem	1839	Bischof	1882
Bien	1840	Bisco	1883
Bier	1841	Bish	1884
Biere	1842	Bisi	1885
Bieri	1843	Bism	1886
Bierm	1844	Biss	1887
Biers	1845	Bissi	1888
Bies	1846	Bist	1889
Biet	1847	Bit	1890
Big	1848	Bitti	1891
Bigg	1849	Bittn	1892
Biggs	1850	Bitts	1893
Bigl	1851	Bix	1894
Bign	1852	Biz	1895
Bih	1853	Bj	1896
Bij	1854	Bla	1897
Bil	1855	Black	1898
Bill	1856	Blackb	1899
Bille	1857	Blacki	1900
Billi	1858	Blackm	1901
Billings	1859	Blackn	1902
Billo	1860	Blackw	1903
Bills	1861	Blad	1904
Bilo	1862	Blae	1905
Bim	1863	Blag	1906
Bin	1864	Blai	1907
Bing	1865	Blair	1908
Bingh	1866	Blais	1909
Bini	1867	Blake	1910
Bink	1868	Blakem	1911
Binn	1869	Blan	1912
Bins	1870	Blanck	1913
Bio	1871	Bland	1914
Bir	1872	Blane	1915
Bird	1873	Blank	1916
Birds	1874	Blanke	1917
Bire	1875	Blanko	1918
Birk	1876	Blas	1919
Birl	1877	Blass	1920
Birm	1878	Blat	1921

Blatt	1922	Board	1965
Blau	1923	Boardm	1966
Blaur	1924	Boas	1967
Blaut	1925	Bob	1968
Blauv	1926	Boc	1969
Blay	1927	Bock	1970
Ble	1928	Bockm	1971
Blee	1029	Bod	1972
Blei	1930	Bode	1973
Bleil	1931	Bodem	1974
Blein	1932	Boden	1975
Bles	1933	Bodi	1976
Blet	1934	Bodk	1977
Bley	1935	Bodo	1978
Bli	1936	Boe	1979
Blim	1937	Boed	1980
Blis	1938	Boeh	1981
Blit	1939	Boehn	1982
Bliv	1940	Boek	1983
Blo	1941	Boel	1984
Block	1942	Boen	1985
Blod	1943	Boer	1986
Blom	1944	Boerk	1987
Blon	1945	Boes	1988
Bloo	1946	Boese	1989
Bloom	1947	Boet	1990
Bloomb	1948	Bof	1991
Bloomf	1949	Bog	1992
Bloomi	1950	Bogart	1993
Blor	1951	Boge	1994
Blos	1952	Bogert	1995
Blot	1953	Bogg	1996
Blu	1954	Bogl	1997
Blum	1955	Boh	1998
Blume	1956	Bohe	1999
Blumens	1957	Bohl	2000
Blumf	1958	Bohlm	2001
Blumm	1959	Bohm	2002
Blun	1960	Bohn	2003
Blus	1961	Bohr	2004
Bly	1962	Boi	2005
Blyn	1963	Bois	2006
Bo	1964	Bok	2007

Bol	2008
Bold	2009
Bole	2010
Bolg	2011
Boli	2012
Boll	2013
Bolle	**2014**
Bolles	2015
Bolli	2016
Bollo	2017
Bolo	2018
Bols	2019
Bolt	2020
Bolton	2021
Bolz	2022
Bom	2023
Bomm	2024
Bon	2025
Bonap	2026
Bonar	2027
Bond	2028
Bondi	2029
Bone	2030
Bonf	2031
Boni	2032
Bonj	2033
Bonn	2034
Bonne	2035
Bonner	2036
Bonno	2037
Bono	2038
Bons	2039
Bont	2040
Bonw	2041
Boo	2042
Book	2043
Booke	2044
Bookm	2045
Books	2046
Boom	2047
Boon	2048
Boor	2049
Boos	2050
Boot	2051
Boothby	2052
Bop	2053
Bor	2054
Bord	2055
Bore	2056
Borg	2057
Borgi	2058
Bori	2059
Bork	2060
Borl	2061
Borm	2062
Born	2063
Borne	2064
Boro	2065
Borr	2066
Bors	2067
Bort	2068
Bos	2069
Bose	2070
Bosi	2071
Boss	2072
Bossi	2073
Bost	2074
Bostw	2075
Bosw	2076
Bot	2077
Bots	2078
Bott	2079
Botti	2080
Botto	2081
Botts	2082
Bou	2083
Boud	2084
Boug	2085
Boul	2086
Boull	2087
Boun	2088
Bour	2089
Bourk	2090
Bourn	2091
Bous	2092
Bout	2093

Bov	2094	Bram	2137
Bow	2095	Bramb	2138
Bowe	2096	Brams	2139
Bowers	2097	Bran	2140
Bowes	2098	Brand	2141
Bowi	2099	Brande	2142
Bowk	2100	Brandi	2143
Bowl	2101	Brando	2144
Bowm	2102	Brandt	2145
Bown	2103	Brane	2146
Bows	2104	Brani	2147
Box	2105	Brann	2148
Boy	2106	Branni	2149
Boyc	2107	Brano	2150
Boyd	2108	Brant	2151
Boye	2109	Bras	2152
Boyl	2110	Brass	2153
Boyle	2111	Brat	2154
Boyls	2112	Brau	2155
Boyn	2113	Braug	2156
Boys	2114	Braun	2157
Boz	2115	Brauns	2158
Bra	2116	Braur	2159
Brac	2117	Braut	2160
Brach	2118	Brav	2161
Brack	2119	Braw	2162
Brad	2120	Bray	2163
Bradd	2121	Braye	2164
Brade	2122	Braz	2165
Bradf	2123	Bre	2166
Bradl	2124	Brear	2167
Bradn	2125	Brec	2168
Brads	2126	Breck	2169
Bradt	2127	Bred	2170
Brady	2128	Bree	2171
Brae	2129	Breg	2172
Brag	2130	Brei	2173
Brah	2131	Brein	2174
Brai	2132	Breis	2175
Brain	2133	Breit	2176
Braine	2134	Breitm	2177
Brais	2135	Brej	2178
Brak	2136	Brem	2179

Bren	2180	Britto	2223
Brene	2181	Bro	2224
Brenn	2182	Broadm	2225
Brenner	2183	Brob	2226
Brent	2184	Broc	2227
Breo	2185	Brocke	2228
Bres	1286	Brocki	2229
Bresn	2187	Brocks	2230
Bress	2188	Brod	2231
Bret	2189	Broder	2232
Brett	2190	Brodi	2233
Breu	2191	Brodm	2234
Brev	2192	Brody	2235
Brew	2193	Broe	2236
Brews	2194	Brog	2237
Brey	2195	Brok	2238
Bri	2196	Brom	2239
Brick	2197	Bromm	2240
Brid	2198	Bron	2241
Bridges	2199	Bronn	2242
Bridgm	2200	Brons	2243
Brie	2201	Broo	2244
Briel	2202	Brookf	2245
Brier	2203	Brookl	2246
Bries	2204	Brooks	2247
Brig	2205	Broom	2248
Brigg	2206	Brop	2249
Bright	2207	Bros	2250
Brigl	2208	Bross	2251
Bril	2209	Brot	2252
Brim	2210	Brou	2253
Brin	2211	Broun	2254
Brine	2212	Brow	2255
Brink	2213	Brown	2256
Brinkm	2214	Browne	2257
Brinn	2215	Brownell	2258
Brio	2216	Browni	2259
Bris	2217	Brownl	2260
Brit	2218	Brows	2261
Brite	2219	Bru	2262
Britt	2220	Bruck	2263
Britte	2221	Brud	2264
Britti	2222	Brue	2265

—C—

Conw	2860	Corp	2903
Coo	2861	Corr	2904
Cooke	2862	Corra	2905
Cool	2863	Corre	2906
Cooley	2864	Corrig	2907
Cooli	2865	Corro	2908
Coom	2866	Cors	2909
Coon	2867	Corse	2910
Coone	2868	Corso	2911
Coons	2869	Cort	2912
Coop	2870	Corte	2913
Cooperm	2871	Corti	2914
Coor	2872	Cortl	2915
Cop	2873	Cory	2916
Copi	2874	Cos	2917
Copl	2875	Cosh	2918
Copp	2876	Cosm	2919
Coppi	2877	Coss	2920
Coppo	2878	Cost	2921
Cor	2879	Coste	2922
Corb	2880	Costi	2923
Corbett	2881	Costo	2924
Corbi	2882	Cot	2925
Corbit	2883	Cott	2926
Corbl	2884	Cotter	2927
Core	2885	Cotti	2928
Cord	2886	Cotto	2929
Cordes	2887	Cottr	2930
Cords	2888	Cou	2931
Core	2889	Coud	2932
Corey	2890	Coug	2933
Corf	2891	Coughlín	2934
Cori	2892	Coul	2935
Cork	2893	Coult	2936
Corl	2894	Coum	2937
Corm	2895	Coun	2938
Corn	2896	Coup	2939
Cornell	2897	Cour	2940
Corner	2898	Court	2941
Corni	2899	Courtn	2942
Cornw	2900	Cous	2943
Cornwell	2901	Cousi	2944
Coro	2902	Cout	2945

Cov	2946	Cred	2989
Covert	2947	Cree	2990
Covi	2948	Creeg	2991
Cow	2949	Creen	2992
Cowd	2950	Creg	2993
Cowe	2951	Crei	2994
Cowi	2952	Crem	2995
Cowl	2953	Crep	2996
Cowm	2954	Cres	2997
Cox	2955	Cress	2998
Coxe	2956	Creu	2999
Coy	2957	Crev	3000
Coyn	2958	Crew	3001
Coz	2959	Cri	3002
Cr	2960	Crid	3003
Crad	2961	Crim	3004
Crag	2962	Crin	3005
Crai	2963	Crip	3006
Craige	2964	Cris	3007
Crain	2965	Crisp	3008
Cral	2966	Crist	3009
Cram	2967	Crit	3010
Cramer	2968	Critt	3011
Cramm	2969	Cro	3012
Cramp	2970	Crock	3013
Cran	2971	Crocket	3014
Crande	2972	Croe	3015
Crane	2973	Crof	3016
Cranf	2974	Crog	3017
Crank	2975	Croh	3018
Crans	2976	Croi	3019
Crap	2977	Crok	3020
Crar	2978	Crol	3021
Cras	2979	Crom	3022
Crat	2980	Cron	3023
Crav	2981	Cronk	3024
Craw	2982	Cronl	3025
Crawf	2983	Croo	3026
Crawl	2984	Crooks	3027
Cray	2985	Crop	3028
Cre	2986	Cros	3029
Cream	2987	Cross	3030
Creas	2988	Crossl	3031

—D—

Dewe	3369	Dille	3412
Dewi	3370	Dilli	3413
Dewo	3371	Dillo	3414
Dews	3372	Dilo	3415
Dex	3373	Dim	3416
Dey	3374	Dime	3417
Deyo	3375	Dimm	3418
Dez	3376	Dimo	3419
Dh	3377	Din	3420
Di	3378	Dine	3421
Diamond	3379	Ding	3422
Dian	3380	Dini	3423
Dib	3381	Dinn	3424
Die	3382	Dins	3425
Dick	3383	Dio	3426
Dicke	3384	Dip	3427
Dieker	3385	Dir	3428
Dickert	3386	Dirk	3429
Dickh	3387	Dis	3430
Dicki	3388	Disc	3431
Dicks	3389	Dise	3432
Did	3390	Dism	3433
Die	3391	Disp	3434
Died	3392	Dist	3435
Dief	3393	Dit	3436
Dieg	3394	Ditt	3437
Dieh	3395	Div	3438
Diek	3396	Dix	3439
Diem	3397	Dixon	3440
Dien	3398	Dla	3441
Dier	3399	Do	3442
Dierk	3400	Dob	3443
Dies	3401	Dobbs	3444
Diet	3402	Dobe	3445
Dietr	3403	Dobl	3446
Dietz	3404	Dobr	3447
Dif	3405	Dobs	3448
Dig	3406	Doc	3449
Digi	3407	Dod	3450
Dik	3408	Dodds	3451
Dil	3409	Dodg	3452
Dilg	3410	Dodi	3453
Dill	3411	Dods	3454

Drap	3541	Dud	3584
Dras	3542	Dudl	3585
Dray	3543	Due	3586
Dre	3544	Duf	3587
Dree	3545	Duffey	3588
Drei	3546	Duffy	3589
Drek	3547	Dufi	3590
Dren	3548	Dug	3591
Dres	3549	Dugg	3592
Dress	3550	Dugl	3593
Dressi	3551	Duh	3594
Dret	3552	Duke	3595
Drew	3553	Dul	3596
Drewe	3554	Dull	3597
Drex	3555	Dum	3598
Drey	3556	Dumm	3599
Dreyf	3557	Dun	3600
Dri	3558	Dunc	3601
Drig	3559	Dund	3602
Dril	3560	Dunh	3603
Dris	3561	Duni	3604
Drisl	3562	Dunk	3605
Drit	3563	Dunl	3606
Dro	3564	Dunle	3607
Drol	3565	Dunlo	3608
Dros	3566	Dunm	3609
Dross	3567	Dunn	3610
Dru	3568	Dunni	3611
Druc	3569	Dunp	3612
Drug	3570	Duns	3613
Drum	3571	Dunt	3614
Drumm	3572	Dup	3615
Drur	3573	Dupo	3616
Dry	3574	Dupr	3617
Dryf	3575	Dur	3618
Du	3576	Durant	3619
Dub	3577	Durb	3620
Dubi	3578	Dure	3621
Dubo	3579	Durf	3622
Dubr	3580	Durh	3623
Duc	3581	Duri	3624
Duck	3582	Durk	3625
Ducl	3583	Durl	3626

—E—

Este	3877	Ever	3893
Esti	3878	Everet	3894
Esto	3879	Evers	3895
Et	3880	Evert	3896
Eti	3881	Evi	3897
Ett	3882	Ew	3898
Ettl	3883	Ewe	3899
Etz	3884	Ewi	3900
Eu	3885	Ex	3901
Eum	3886	Exc	3902
Eus	3887	Exl	3903
Ev	3888	Ey	3904
Evans	3889	Eyr	3905
Evar	3890	Eys	3906
Eve	3891	Eyt	3907
Even	3892	Ez	3908

—F—

Fa	3909	Fann	3932
Fab	3910	Fans	3933
Fabi	3911	Fap	3934
Fac	3912	Far	3935
Fad	3913	Fard	3936
Fae	3914	Fari	3937
Fag	3915	Farl	3938
Fagg	3916	Farm	3939
Fah	3917	Farn	3940
Fai	3918	Farnh	3941
Fair	3919	Farq	3942
Faire	3920	Farr	3943
Fairf	3921	Farra	3944
Fairl	3922	Farre	3945
Fais	3923	Farren	3946
Fait	3924	Farri	3947
Fal	3925	Farro	3948
Falk	3926	Fas	3949
Falke	3927	Fast	3950
Fall	3928	Fau	3951
Fallo	3929	Faus	3952
Fam	3930	Fav	3953
Fan	3931	Faw	3954

Fay	3955	Fes	3998
Fea	3956	Fess	3999
Feas	3957	Fet	4000
Fec	3958	Fett	4001
Fed	3959	Fetti	4002
Fee	3960	Feu	4003
Feg	3961	Feug	4004
Fei	3962	Fey	4005
Feig	3963	Fi	4006
Feil	3964	Fic	4007
Fein	3965	Fick	4008
Feis	3966	Fid	4009
Feit	3967	Fie	4010
Fel	3968	Fieg	4011
Feldm	3969	Field	4012
Feldo	3970	Fieldi	4013
Fele	3971	Fields	4014
Fell	3972	Fien	4015
Fellm	3973	Fies	4016
Feln	3974	Fife	4017
Felt	3975	Fig	4018
Fen	3976	Fil	4019
Fene	3977	File	4020
Fenl	3978	Fili	4021
Fenn	3979	Fill	4022
Fennel	3980	Fillm	4023
Fenni	3981	Fim	4024
Fens	3982	Fin	4025
Fent	3983	Finck	4026
Fer	3984	Fincke	4027
Ferd	3985	Find	4028
Ferg	3986	Findl	4029
Feri	3987	Fine	4030
Fern	3988	Fineg	4031
Fernan	3989	Finel	4032
Fernb	3990	Fing	4033
Ferns	3991	Fink	4034
Ferr	3992	Finke	4035
Ferrer	3993	Finkelm	4036
Ferri	3994	Finken	4037
Ferris	3995	Finkle	4038
Ferry	3996	Finl	4039
Fert	3997	Finn	4040

Finne	4041	Flanni	4084
Finnel	4042	Flas	4085
Finni	4043	Flat	4086
Finno	4044	Flau	4087
Fins	4045	Flaw	4088
Fio	4046	Fle	4089
Fir	4047	Fleck	4090
Firm	4048	Flee	4091
Firs	4049	Flei	4092
Firt	4050	Fleis	4093
Fis	4051	Fleish	4094
Fisch	4052	Flem	4095
Fischl	4053	Flemm	4096
Fish	4054	Flen	4097
Fishe	4055	Fles	4098
Fisher	4056	Flet	4099
Fishi	4057	Fli	4100
Fisk	4058	Flie	4101
Fiske	4059	Flig	4102
Fiss	4060	Flin	4103
Fit	4061	Flint	4104
Fite	4062	Flo	4105
Fitz	4063	Flod	4106
Fitzg	4064	Floh	4107
Fitzgr	4065	Flon	4108
Fitzh	4066	Flor	4109
Fitzm	4067	Florent	4110
Fitzp	4068	Flori	4111
Fiv	4069	Florm	4112
Fix	4070	Flos	4113
Fl	4071	Flow	4114
Flach	4072	Floy	4115
Flack	4073	Flu	4116
Flad	4074	Fluo	4117
Flag	4075	Fly	4118
Flagg	4076	Fo	4119
Flah	4077	Foe	4120
Flai	4078	Foer	4121
Flam	4079	Fog	4122
Flan	4080	Foge	4123
Fland	4081	Fogg	4124
Flani	4082	Foh	4125
Flann	4083	Fol	4126

F—Continued.

—G—

Gag	4292	Garr	4335
Gah	4293	Garrett	4336
Gai	4294	Garri	4337
Gain	4295	Garris	4338
Gair	4296	Garrit	4339
Gal	4297	Garro	4340
Galb	4298	Gars	4341
Gale	4299	Gart	4342
Gales	4300	Garth	4343
Gali	4301	Gartn	4344
Gall	4302	Garv	4345
Gallan	4303	Garw	4346
Galle	4304	Gas	4347
Galli	4305	Gask	4348
Gallo	4306	Gass	4349
Gallu	4307	Gast	4350
Galm	4308	Gat	4351
Galp	4309	Gates	4352
Galv	4310	Gatt	4353
Galw	4311	Gau	4354
Gam	4312	Gaul	4355
Gambl	4313	Gaus	4356
Game	4314	Gant	4357
Gan	4315	Gav	4358
Gane	4316	Gavi	4359
Gani	4317	Gaw	4360
Gann	4318	Gay	4361
Gans	4319	Gayn	4362
Gant	4320	Gaz	4363
Ganz	4321	Gea	4364
Gar	4322	Gear	4365
Garb	4323	Geary	4366
Garc	4324	Geb	4367
Gard	4325	Gebh	4368
Gardi	4326	Gec	4369
Gardn	4327	Ged	4370
Gare	4328	Gee	4371
Garf	4329	Geer	4372
Gari	4330	Gef	4373
Garl	4331	Geg	4374
Garm	4332	Geh	4375
Garn	4333	Gehl	4376
Garo	4334	Gei	4377

Girl	4464	Godw	4507
Gis	4465	Goe	4508
Git	4466	Goec	4509
Gitt	4467	Goel	4510
Giu	4468	Goem	4511
Giv	4469	Goep	4512
Gla	4470	Goer	4513
Glad	4471	Goet	4514
Glar	4472	Goetz	4515
Glas	4473	Gof	4516
Glasg	4474	Gog	4517
Glass	4475	Goh	4518
Glasse	4476	Goi	4519
Glassf	4477	Gol	4520
Glassm	4478	Gold	4521
Glat	4479	Golde	4522
Glau	4480	Goldf	4523
Glaz	4481	Goldg	4524
Gle	4482	Goldi	4525
Glei	4483	Goldm	4526
Glen	4484	Goldn	4527
Glenn	4485	Golds	4528
Gles	4486	Goldst	4529
Gli	4487	Goldw	4530
Glid	4488	Gole	4531
Glin	4489	Goll	4532
Glo	4490	Golle	4533
Gloc	4491	Gollo	4534
Gloe	4492	Gom	4535
Glor	4493	Gomm	4536
Glov	4494	Gon	4537
Glu	4495	Goo	4538
Gly	4496	Good	4539
Gm	4497	Goode	4540
Gn	4498	Goodf	4541
Go	4490	Goodh	4542
Gob	4500	Goodk	4543
Goc	4501	Goodm	4544
God	4502	Goodn	4545
Godd	4503	Goodr	4546
Godf	4504	Goods	4547
Godi	4505	Goodw	4548
Godn	4506	Goody	4549

Goos	4550	Grav	4593
Gor	4551	Gray	4594
Gore	4552	Grayb	4595
Gorf	4553	Graz	4596
Gorh	4554	Grea	4597
Gorm	4555	Grear	4598
Gorml	4556	Great	4599
Gorr	4557	Greater	4600
Gort	4558	Greb	4601
Gos	4559	Grec	4602
Goss	4560	Gree	4603
Got	4561	Greel	4604
Gott	4562	Green	4605
Gottl	4563	Greena	4606
Gotts	4564	Greenbe	4607
Gou	4565	Greenbl	4608
Goul	4566	Greenbo	4609
Goulde	4567	Greene	4610
Gour	4568	Greeneb	4611
Gov	4569	Greenf	4612
Gow	4570	Greenh	4613
Gra	4571	Greeni	4614
Grac	4572	Greenm	4615
Grad	4573	Greens	4616
Grae	4574	Greenw	4617
Graf	4575	Greer	4618
Graft	4576	Gref	4619
Grah	4577	Greg	4620
Grai	4578	Grego	4621
Gram	4579	Gregori	4622
Gran	4580	Gregory	4623
Grand	4581	Grei	4624
Grane	4582	Greig	4625
Grani	4583	Grein	4626
Grann	4584	Greis	4627
Grant	4585	Greiv	4628
Grap	4586	Grem	4629
Gras	4587	Gren	4630
Grass	4588	Gres	4631
Grat	4589	Gress	4632
Gratt	4590	Gret	4633
Grau	4591	Greu	4634
Graul	4592	Grev	4635

Gus	4722	Gutt	4728
Gust	4723	Guttm	4729
Gut	4724	Guy	4730
Guth	4725	Gwa	4731
Guthr	4726	Gwy	4732
Gutm	4727	Gy	4733

—H—

Ha	4734	Hai	4767
Haag	4735	Haight	4768
Haak	4736	Hail	4769
Hɛar	4737	Hain	4770
Haas	4738	Hair	4771
Hab	4739	Haj	4772
Habe	4740	Hal	4773
Habi	4741	Hale	4774
Hac	4742	Halem	4775
Hack	4743	Half	4776
Hacker	4744	Hall	4777
Hacket	4745	Halla	4778
Hackl	4746	Halle	4779
Had	4747	Hallem	4780
Hade	4748	Halli	4781
Hadl	4749	Hallig	4782
Hae	4750	Hallo	4783
Haeg	4751	Halls	4784
Haen	4752	Halm	4785
Haes	4753	Halp	4786
Haf	4754	Halpin	4787
Hafte	4755	Hals	4788
Hafk	4756	Halsted	4789
Hag	4757	Halter	4790
Hage	4758	Ham	4791
Hagem	4759	Hamb	4792
Hagen	4760	Hambu	4793
Hager	4761	Hame	4794
Hagg	4762	Hami	4795
Hago	4763	Hamilton	4796
Hah	4764	Hamin	4797
Hahn	4765	Hamli	4798
Hahne	4766	Hamm	4799

Hassl	4886	Hazen	4929
Hast	4887	Hazl	4930
Hat	4888	Hazz	4931
Hath	4889	Hea	4932
Hati	4890	Heal	4933
Hatt	4891	Heale	4934
Hatto	4892	Heali	4935
Hau	4893	Healy	4936
Haue	4894	Hean	4937
Haug	4895	Hear	4938
Haugh	4896	Heat	4939
Haupt	4897	Heath	4940
Haupte	**4898**	Heato	4941
Haus	4899	Heav	4942
Hause	4900	Heb	4943
Haush	4901	Hebe	4944
Hausm	4902	Hebi	4945
Hausn	4903	Hebr	4946
Hauss	4904	Hec	4947
Haut	4905	Heck	4948
Hav	4906	Hecker	4949
Have	4907	Hecki	4950
Haven	4908	Heckm	4951
Haver	4909	Hecks	4952
Havi	4910	Hed	4953
Haw	4911	Hedg	4954
Hawk	4912	Hedi	4955
Hawl	4913	Hee	4956
Hawt	4914	Heel	4957
Hax	4915	Heer	4958
Hay	4916	Hef	4959
Hayd	4917	Heff	4960
Haye	4918	Heffl	4961
Hayl	4919	Hefn	4962
Haym	4920	Heg	4963
Hayn	4921	Hegg	4964
Haynes	4922	Heh	4965
Hays	4923	Hei	4966
Hayt	4924	Heidel	4967
Haywa	4925	Heidi	4968
Haywo	4926	Heidl	4969
Haz	4927	Heif	4970
Haze	4928	Heig	4971

Heil	4972	Helv	5015
Heilb	4973	Hem	5016
Heilbru	4974	Hemi	5017
Heile	4975	Hemm	5018
Heilm	4976	Hemmer	5019
Heim	4977	Hemmi	5020
Heimb	4978	Hemp	5021
Heime	4979	Hemps	5022
Heiml	4980	Hen	5023
Hein	4981	Henc	5024
Heina	4982	Hend	5025
Heine	4983	Hendr	5026
Heinem	4984	Hend'Ks'n	5027
Heinen	4985	Hene	5028
Heini	4986	Heng	5029
Heink	4987	Heni	5030
Heinm	4988	Henk	5031
Heins	4989	Henl	5032
Heinsi	4990	Henn	5033
Heint	4991	Henne	5034
Heinz	4992	Hennes	5035
Heip	4993	Hennessy	5036
Heis	4994	Henni	5037
Heisl	4995	Hennin	5038
Heiss	4996	Hennings	5039
Heit	4997	Heno	5040
Heitm	4998	Henri	5041
Hel	4999	Henrie	5042
Held	5000	Henry	5043
Hele	5001	Hens	5044
Helf	5002	Hensi	5045
Helfo	5003	Henso	5046
Hell	5004	Hent	5047
Heller	5005	Henw	5048
Hellf	5006	Hep	5049
Hellm	5007	Hepi	5050
Hellr	5008	Hepp	5051
Helm	5009	Her	5052
Helme	5010	Herb	5053
Helmi	5011	Herbert	5054
Helms	5012	Herbi	5055
Help	5013	Herbst	5056
Helr	5014	Herc	5057

Herd	5058	Hessl	5101
Here	5059	Hessm	5102
Heri	5060	Het	5103
Herk	5061	Hett	5104
Herl	5062	Hetz	5105
Herm	5063	Heu	5106
Hermann	5064	Heum	5107
Hermanns	5065	Heus	5108
Herme	5066	Hev	5109
Hern	5067	Hew	5110
Herne	5068	Hewi	5111
Hero	5069	Hewl	5112
Heron	5070	Hex	5113
Herp	5071	Hey	5114
Herr	5072	Heyd	5115
Herre	5073	Heydo	5116
Herri	5074	Heye	5117
Herrl	5075	Heym	5118
Herrm	5076	Heyn	5119
Herrmann	5077	Heyr	5120
Herro	5078	Heyw	5121
Hers	5079	Heyz	5122
Herschi	5080	Hib	5123
Herschu	5081	Hibbe	5124
Herse	5082	Hic	5125
Hersh	5083	Hickey	5126
Hersk	5084	Hicki	5127
Hert	5085	Hickm	5128
Hertf	5086	Hicko	5129
Herts	5087	Hicks	5130
Hertz	5088	Hickson	5131
Hertzb	5089	Hid	5132
Herv	5090	Hie	5133
Herw	5091	Hig	5134
Herz	5092	Higg	5135
Herze	5093	Higgs	5136
Herzi	5094	High	5137
Herzo	5095	Higl	5138
Hes	5096	Hil	5139
Hess	5097	Hild	5140
Hesse	5098	Hildeb'dt	5141
Hellel	5099	Hilder	5142
Hessi	5100	Hildg	5143

Hoey	5230	Holmf	5273
Hof	5231	Holo	5274
Hofe	5232	Hols	5275
Hoff	5233	Holst	5276
Hoffm	5234	Holt	5277
Hoffmann	5235	Holte	5278
Hoffs	5236	Holth	5279
Hofh	5237	Holto	5280
Hofm	5238	Holtz	5281
Hofme	5239	Holtze	5282
Hofs	5240	Holu	5283
Hog	5241	Holy	5284
Hoge	5242	Holz	5285
Hogg	5243	Holzd	5286
Hogi	5244	Holzh	5287
Hoh	5245	Holzm	5288
Hohl	5246	Holzn	5289
Hohm	5247	Hom	5290
Hoho	5248	Home	5291
Hoi	5249	Homer	5292
Hok	5250	Homi	5293
Hol	5251	Homo	5294
Holb	5252	Hon	5295
Holbr	5253	Hone	5296
Hole	5254	Hones	5297
Hold	5255	Honi	5298
Holder	5256	Honn	5299
Holdi	5257	Hoo	5300
Hole	5258	Hoog	5301
Holi	5259	Hook	5302
Holl	5260	Hool	5303
Holle	5261	Hoop	5304
Holler	5262	Hoops	5305
Hoilet	5263	Hoor	5306
Holli	5264	Hoov	5307
Hollings	5265	Hop	5308
Hollis	5266	Hopf	5309
Hollm	5267	Hopk	5310
Hollo	5268	Hopko	5311
Holls	5269	Hopp	5312
Holly	5270	Hopper	5313
Holm	5271	Hops	5314
Holme	5272	Hor	5315

Hult	5402	Hurs	5431
Hum	5403	Hurt	5432
Humbo	5404	Hus	5433
Hume	5405	Hush	5434
Hummel	5406	Huss	5435
Humm	5407	Hust	5436
Humphre	5408	Husti	5437
Humphri	5409	Hut	5438
Huna	5410	Hutchinson	5439
Hune	5411	Hutchison	5440
Huni	5412	Huth	5441
Hunn	5413	Hutl	5442
Huno	5414	Hutt	5443
Hunt	5415	Hutto	5444
Hunter	5416	Hutw	5445
Hunting	5417	Hux	5446
Hunt'gt'n	5418	Huy	5447
Huntl	5419	Hv	5448
Hunts	5420	Hya	5449
Hup	5421	Hyat	5450
Hupp	5422	Hyde	5451
Hur	5423	Hydr	5452
Hurd	5424	Hyer	5453
Hure	5425	Hyg	5454
Hurl	5426	Hyl	5455
Hurle	5427	Hym	5456
Hurli	5428	Hyn	5457
Hurm	5429	Hys	5458
Hurr	5430		

—I—

Ia	5459	Ige	5469
Ib	5460	Igl	5470
Ic	5461	Ign	5471
Ida	5462	Ih	5472
Ide	5463	Ik	5473
Idi	5464	Il	5474
Idl	5465	Ill	5475
Ie	5466	Ils	5476
If	5467	Ima	5477
Iga	5468	Imm	5478

73

Latt	5721	Lebo	5764
Latu	5722	Lebr	5765
Lau	5723	Lec	5766
Lauc	5724	Leck	5767
Laue	5725	Lecl	5768
Lauf	5726	Leco	5769
Laug	5727	Led	5770
Laui	5728	Ledi	5771
Laun	5729	Ledu	5772
Laur	5730	Lee	5773
Laut	5731	Leeb	5774
Lauth	5732	Leed	5775
Laux	5733	Leem	5776
Lav	5734	Leer	5777
Laven	5735	Lees	5778
Laver	5736	Lef	5779
Lavi	5737	Leff	5780
Law	5738	Leffi	5781
Lawl	5739	Lefi	5782
Lawles	5740	Leg	5783
Lawlo	5741	Legg	5784
Lawm	5742	Legh	5785
Lawr	5743	Leh	5786
Laws	5744	Lehm	5787
Lawt	5745	Lehn	5788
Lawy	5746	Lehr	5789
Lax	5747	Leib	5790
Lay	5748	Leic	5791
Laym	5749	Leid	5792
Laz	5750	Leif	5793
Lea	5751	Leig	5794
Lead	5752	Leim	5795
Leaf	5753	Lein	5796
Leah	5754	Leip	5797
Leak	5755	Leis	5798
Leam	5756	Leiss	5799
Lear	5757	Leit	5800
Leary	5758	Lej	5801
Leas	5759	Lel	5802
Leav	5760	Lell	5803
Leay	5761	Lem	5804
Leb	5762	Lemb	5805
Lebi	5763	Lemi	5806

Lio	5893
Lip	5894
Lipp	5895
Lippi	5896
Lippm	5897
Lips	5898
Lis	5899
Liss	5900
Lisso	5901
Lit	5902
Litt	5903
Little	5904
Littm	5905
Liv	5906
Livi	5907
Livi'gstone	5908
Liz	5909
Ll	5910
Lloyd	5911
Loa	5912
Lobes	5913
Loc	5914
Lock	5915
Locke	5916
Lockh	5917
Lockw	5918
Locky	5919
Lod	5920
Loe	5921
Loebe	5922
Loef	5923
Loeh	5924
Loes	5925
Loess	5926
Loew	5927
Loewen	5928
Loewent	5929
Loewi	5930
Lof	5931
Log	5932
Logg	5933
Loh	5934
Lohmann	5935
Lohr	5936
Lohs	5937
Loi	5938
Loid	5939
Lok	5940
Lom	5941
Lon	5942
Long	5943
Longf	5944
Longl	5945
Longs	5946
Lons	5947
Loo	5948
Loom	5949
Loos	5950
Lop	5951
Lor	5952
Lord	5953
Lore	5954
Lori	5955
Lorim	5956
Lort	5957
Los	5958
Lot	5959
Lott	5960
Lotti	5961
Lou	5962
Loug	5963
Loughr	5964
Loughrn	5965
Louis	5966
Loum	5967
Loup	5968
Lova	5969
Love	5970
Lovel	5971
Lovell	5972
Lovem	5973
Lovi	5974
Low	5975
Lowb	5976
Lowe	5977
Lowel	5978

Lowen	5979	Lum	6008
Lowens	5980	Luna	6009
Lowent	5981	Lune	6010
Lower	5982	Luni	6011
Lowi	5983	Luno	6012
Lown	5984	Lup	6013
Lowr	5985	Luq	6014
Loy	5986	Lur	6015
Loz	5987	Lus	6016
Lu	5988	Lusk	6017
Lube	5989	Lust	6018
Lubi	5990	Lut	6019
Lubo	5991	Luth	6020
Luc	5992	Lutt	6021
Luce	5993	Lutz	6022
Luci	5994	Lux	6023
Luck	5995	Luy	6024
Lud	5996	Lya	6025
Ludi	5997	Lyd	6026
Ludlo	5998	Lye	6027
Ludm	5999	Lyi	6028
Ludw	6000	Lym	6029
Lue	6001	Lyn	6030
Luf	6002	Lynch	6031
Lug	6003	Lynd	6032
Luh	6004	Lyne	6033
Lui	6005	Lynn	6034
Luk	6006	Lyo	6035
Lul	6007	Lyr	6036

—M—

Maa	6037	Macalp	6047
Mab	6038	Macalu	6048
Mabi	6039	Macana	6049
Maca	6040	Macane	6050
Macaf	6041	Macard	6051
Macala	6042	Macare	6052
Macaleer	6043	Macart	6053
Macali	6044	Macaula	6054
Macall	6045	Macaule	6055
Macalo	6046	Macauli	6056

Macav	6057	Maccli	6100
Macba	6058	Macclo	6101
Macbe	6059	Macclu	6102
Macbr	6060	Macclurg	6103
Macbri	6061	M'ccluskey	6104
Macbro	6062	Macclusky	6105
Macbu	6063	Macco	6106
Maccab	6064	Maccoll	6107
Maccad	6065	Maccollu	6108
Maccaff'ty	6066	Maccom	6109
Maccaffery	6067	Maccon	6110
Maccaffrey	6068	Macconno	6111
Maccag	6069	Macconv	6112
Maccah	6070	Maccoo	6113
Maccai	6071	Maccool	6114
Maccal	6072	M'ccormack	6115
Maccali	6073	M'ccormick	6116
Maccallu	6074	Maccort	6117
Maccalm	6075	Maccos	6118
Maccan	6076	Maccou	6119
Maccann	6077	Maccow	6120
Maccar	6078	Maccoy	6121
Maccarr	6079	Maccrac	6122
Maccarri	6080	Maccrai	6123
Maccarro	6081	Maccrea	6124
Maccart	6082	Maccred	6125
Maccarthy	6083	Maccree	6126
Maccarti	6084	Maccri	6127
Maccarty	6085	Maccro	6128
Macceas	6086	Maccrud	6129
Maccaud	6087	Maccu	6130
Maccauley	6088	Maccul	6131
Maccaus	6089	Maccullo	6132
Macch	6090	M'cc'lough	6133
Maccl	6091	Maccullum	6134
Macclane	6092	Maccum	6135
Macclat	6093	Maccun	6136
Macclav	6094	Maccur	6137
Macclean	6095	Macceus	6138
Maccleary	6096	Maccut	6139
Macclellan	6097	Macda	6140
Macclen	6098	M'cderm'tt	6141
M'cclennen	6099	Macdev	6142

Macdonal	6143	Macgl	6186
M'cdonnell	6144	Macgli	6187
M'cdon'gh	6145	Macglo	6188
Macdor	6146	Macglon	6189
Macdou	6147	Macgly	6190
Macdu	6148	Macgo	6191
Mace	6149	Macgol	6192
Macel	6150	Macgon	6193
Macell	6151	Macgor	6194
Macelroy	6152	Macgou	6195
Macelv	6153	Macgov	6196
Macelw	6154	Macgow	6197
Macena	6155	Macgown	6198
Macenr	6156	Macgr	6199
Macente	6157	Macgran	6200
Macentyre	6158	Macgrath	6201
Macer	6159	Macgraw	6202
Maceva	6160	Macgre	6203
Macevi	6161	Macgreg	6204
Macevo	6162	Macgro	6205
Macew	6163	Macgror	6206
Macfadden	6164	Macgru	6207
Macfal	6165	Macguc	6208
M'cfarland	6166	Macgui	6209
M'cfarlane	6167	Macguire	6210
Macfe	6168	Macguirk	6211
Macga	6169	Macgur	6212
Macgan	6170	Macgus	6213
Macgar	6171	Macha	6214
Macgarry	6172	Mache	6215
Macgarv	6173	Machi	6216
Macgau	6174	Machu	6217
Macge	6175	Macil	6218
Macgeo	6176	Macilr	6219
Macger	6177	Macilv	6220
Macgi	6178	Macin	6221
Macgill	6179	Macinn	6222
Macgin	6180	Macint	6223
Macginn	6181	Macinty	6224
Macginni	6182	Maciv	6225
Macgint	6183	Mack	6226
Macgir	6184	Mackay	6227
Macgiv	6185	Macke	6228

Mackeever	6229	Macmu	6272
Mackeg	6230	Macmullen	6273
Mackel	6231	Macmur	6274
Macken	6232	Macnab	6275
Mackenz	6233	Macnair	6276
Mackeo	6234	Macnally	6277
Mackeon	6235	M'cnamara	6278
Macker	6236	Macnamee	6279
Mackes	6237	Macnan	6280
Mackev	6238	Macnau	6281
Mackew	6239	Macne	6282
Macki	6240	Macneil	6283
Mackie	6241	Macneill	6284
Mackil	6242	Macneir	6285
Mackim	6243	Macnel	6286
Mackin	6244	Macnet	6287
Mackinn	6245	Macnich	6288
Mackir	6246	Macnico	6289
Mackn	6247	Macnie	6290
Macko	6248	Macnif	6291
Macku	6249	Macnu	6292
Mael	6250	Maco	6293
Maclan	6251	Macp	6294
Maclar	6252	Macpe	6295
M'claughlin	6253	Macph	6296
Macle	6254	Macpi	6297
Maclee	6255	Macqua	6298
Maclel	6256	Macqui	6299
Maclen	6257	Macra	6300
Macleo	6258	Macri	6301
Macler	6259	Macsh	6302
Macli	6260	Macso	6303
M'clo'ghlin	6261	Macsw	6304
Macma	6262	Macta	6305
Macman	6263	Macte	6306
Macmanus	6264	Macti	6307
Macmas	6265	Macva	6308
Macme	6266	Macvi	6309
Macmi	6267	Macwa	6310
Macmille	6268	Macwi	6311
Macmilli	6269	Mada	6312
Macmin	6270	Madde	6313
Macmo	6271	Maddo	6314

Made	6315	Malk	6358
Madg	6316	Mall	6359
Madi	6317	Malli	6360
Madison	6318	Mallo	6361
Madl	6319	Mallory	6362
Mads	6320	Malloy	6363
Mae	6321	Malm	6364
Maf	6322	Malo	6365
Mag	6323	Maloney	6366
Mage	6324	Maloy	6367
Magg	6325	Malr	6368
Magi	6326	Malt	6369
Magin	6327	Mam	6370
Magl	6328	Man	6371
Magna	6329	Manc	6372
Magne	6330	Mand	6373
Magnu	6331	Mandi	6374
Mago	6332	Mando	6375
Magra	6333	Mane	6376
Magri	6334	Manf	6377
Magu	6335	Mang	6378
Maha	6336	Mange	6379
Mahe	6337	Mangi	6380
Mahn	6338	Mango	6381
Mahom	6339	Manh	6382
Mahon	6340	Mani	6383
Mahony	6341	Mank	6384
Mahr	6342	Manl	6385
Mai	6343	Mann	6386
Maier	6344	Manne	6387
Mail	6345	Manni	6388
Maill	6346	Mano	6389
Maim	6347	Mans	6390
Main	6348	Mant	6391
Mains	6349	Manu	6392
Mair	6350	Many	6393
Mait	6351	Map	6394
Maj	6352	Mar	6395
Mak	6353	Marb	6396
Mal	6354	Marc	6397
Mald	6355	Marci	6398
Male	6356	Marco	6399
Mali	6357	Marcu	6400

Mard	6401	Masters	6444
Mare	6402	Masti	6445
Marg	6403	Mat	6446
Mari	6404	Math	6447
Marin	6405	Mathes	6448
Marion	6406	Mathew	5449
Mark	6407	Mathi	6450
Marke	6408	Mati	6451
Markh	6409	Mato	6452
Markl	6410	Matt	6453
Marks	6411	Matthews	6454
Marku	6412	Matthi	6455
Marl	6413	Matti	6456
Marm	6414	Matto	6457
Maro	6415	Matz	6458
Marq	6416	Mau	6459
Marr	6417	Maul	6460
Marre	6418	Maur	6461
Marri	6419	Mav	6462
Marro	6420	Maw	6463
Mars	6421	Max	6464
Marsd	6422	Maxw	6465
Marsh	6423	May	6466
Marshall	6424	Maye	6467
Marsi	6425	Mayf	6468
Marst	6426	Mayl	6469
Mart	6427	Mayn	6470
Martens	6428	Mayo	6471
Marti	6429	Mays	6472
Marto	6430	Maz	6473
Marty	6431	Me	6474
Marv	6432	Mead	6475
Marx	6433	Meag	6476
Mary	6434	Meak	6477
Mas	6435	Mean	6478
Mase	6436	Mear	6479
Masi	6437	Mee	6480
Maso	6438	Meda	6481
Mass	6439	Mede	6482
Masse	6440	Medi	6483
Massi	6441	Medo	6484
Masso	6442	Mee	6485
Mast	6443	Meek	6486

Meg	6487	Merk	6530
Meh	6488	Merl	6531
Mehm	6489	Merr	6532
Mehr	6490	Merrill	6533
Mei	6491	Merrim	6534
Meig	6492	Merrit	6535
Meik	6493	Merro	6536
Mein	6494	Mers	6537
Meir	6495	Mert	6538
Meis	6496	Merv	6539
Meiss	6497	Merw	6540
Meit	**6498**	Mes	6541
Mej	6499	Mess	6542
Mel	6500	Messi	6543
Mele	6501	Messm	6544
Meli	6502	Mest	6545
Mell	6503	Met	6546
Melli	6504	Metc	6547
Mello	6505	Meth	6548
Meln	6506	Metr	6549
Melo	6507	Mett	6550
Melt	6508	Metz	6551
Melv	6509	Metzg	6552
Melz	6510	Metzi	6553
Mem	6511	Meu	6554
Men	6512	Mew	6555
Mend	6513	Mex	6556
Mendo	6514	Mey	6557
Mene	6515	Meyers	6558
Meng	6516	Meyf	6559
Menh	6517	Meyr	6560
Menk	6518	Mez	6561
Menn	6519	Mia	6562
Meno	6520	Mic	6563
Ment	6521	Michaels	6564
Menz	6522	Michal	6565
Meo	6523	Michel	6566
Mer	6524	Michels	6567
Mercer	6525	Michi	6568
Merci	6526	Mid	6569
Mere	6527	Middled	6570
Merg	6528	Middlet	6571
Meri	6529	Midg	6572

Mie	6573	Missi	6616
Mier	6574	Misso	6617
Miet	6575	Mit	6618
Mig	6576	Mite	6619
Mih	6577	Mitt	6620
Mik	6578	Mix	6621
Mil	6579	Moa	6622
Mild	6580	Moc	6623
Mile	6581	Mod	6624
Mili	6582	Moe	6625
Mill	6583	Moen	6626
Miller	6584	Moer	6627
Milles	6585	Moes	6628
Milli	6586	Mof	6629
Millin	6587	Moffi	6630
Milln	6588	Mog	6631
Mills	6589	Moh	6632
Milm	6590	Mohr	6633
Miln	6591	Moi	6634
Milo	6592	Mol	6635
Mils	6593	Mole	6636
Milt	6594	Moli	6637
Milw	6595	Moll	6638
Mim	6596	Molle	6639
Min	6597	Molli	6640
Mind	6598	Mollo	6641
Mine	6599	Molo	6642
Minera	6600	Molt	6643
Ming	6601	Mom	6644
Mini	6602	Mon	6645
Mink	6603	Monah	6646
Minn	6604	Monar	6647
Mino	6605	Monc	6648
Minr	6606	Mond	6649
Mint	6607	Mone	6650
Mintz	6608	Monf	6651
Mir	6609	Mong	6652
Mire	6610	Monh	6653
Miro	6611	Monk	6654
Mis	6612	Monn	6655
Mise	6613	Monr	6656
Misi	6614	Mons	6657
Miss	6615	Mont	6658

Montan	6659	Morto	6702
Montc	6660	Mos	6703
Monte	6661	Mosc	6704
Montf	6662	Mose	6705
Montg	6663	Moses	6706
Month	6664	Mosh	6707
Monti	6665	Mosi	6708
Montr	6666	Mosk	6709
Monu	6667	Mosl	6710
Moo	6668	Moss	6711
Moog	6669	Mossl	6712
Moon	6670	Mosso	6713
Moor	6671	Mot	6714
Moorh	6672	Mott	6715
Moos	6673	Mou	6716
Mor	6674	Moun	6717
Moran	6675	Mountain	6718
Mord	6676	Mouq	6719
More	6677	Mous	6720
Morel	6678	Mow	6721
Moren	6679	Mox	6722
Moret	6680	Moy	6723
Morf	6681	Moz	6724
Morga	6682	Muc	6725
Morge	6683	Mud	6726
Morh	6684	Mue	6727
Mori	6685	Muel	6728
Morie	6686	Muem	6729
Morio	6687	Muer	6730
Morit	6688	Muf	6731
Morj	6689	Mug	6732
Morl	6690	Muh	6733
Morm	6691	Mui	6734
Morn	6692	Mul	6735
Moro	6693	Mule	6736
Morr	6694	Mulf	6737
Morri	6695	Mulg	6738
Morris	6696	Mulh	6739
Morrisa	6697	Mulhe	6740
Morrison	6698	Mulho	6741
Morro	6699	Muli	6742
Mors	6700	Mull	6743
Mort	6701	Mullan	6744

Mulle	6745	Muri	6766
Muller	6746	Murl	6767
Mulli	6747	Murphy	6768
Mullin	6748	Murray	6769
Mullo	6749	Murre	6770
Mulr	6750	Murt	6771
Muls	6751	Musa	6772
Mulv	6752	Muse	6773
Mum	6753	Musi	6774
Mun	6754	Musk	6775
Mundo	6755	Muss	6776
Mung	6756	Must	6777
Muni	6757	Mut	6778
Munk	6758	Mutu	6779
Munn	6759	Mutz	6780
Munr	6760	Muz	6781
Muns	6761	My	6782
Munst	6762	Myers	6783
Munt	6763	Myg	6784
Mur	6764	Myl	6785
Murd	6765	Myr	6786

—N—

Na	6787	Nar	6805
Nae	6788	Nari	6806
Nad	6789	Nas	6807
Nadl	6790	Nasi	6808
Nae	6791	Nass	6809
Naf	6792	Nasse	6810
Nag	6793	Nast	6811
Nagi	6794	Nat	6812
Nago	6795	Nath	6813
Nah	6796	Nathans	6814
Nai	6797	Nati	6815
Nal	6798	Natt	6816
Nam	6799	Nau	6817
Nan	6800	Naug	6818
Nap	6801	Naum	6819
Napl	6802	Naun	6820
Napoleor	6803	Nav	6821
Napoli	6804	Nay	6822

—O—

Owi	7073	Oy	7076
Ox	7074	Oz	7077
Oxl	7075		

—P—

Pa	7078	Papi	7114
Pab	7079	Papp	7115
Pac	7080	Par	7116
Pach	7081	Pard	7117
Paci	7082	Pardi	7118
Pack	7083	Pare	7119
Pad	7084	Pari	7120
Padi	7085	Park	7121
Pae	7086	Parker	7122
Paf	7087	Parkh	7123
Pag	7088	Parki	7124
Page	7089	Parl	7125
Pagi	7090	Parm	7126
Pah	7091	Parn	7127
Pai	7092	Parr	7128
Pain	7093	Parre	7129
Paint	7094	Parri	7130
Pak	7095	Parro	7131
Pal	7096	Parry	7132
Pali	7097	Parse	7133
Pall	7098	Parso	7134
Palm	7099	Parta	7135
Palme	7100	Party	7136
Palmi	7101	Pas	7137
Palo	7102	Pask	7138
Palu	7103	Pass	7139
Pam	7104	Past	7140
Pan	7105	Pasti	7141
Panc	7106	Pat	7142
Pane	7107	Paterson	7143
Pang	7108	Pato	7144
Panne	7109	Patr	7145
Pant	7110	Patt	7146
Pao	7111	Patterson	7147
Pap	7112	Patti	7148
Pape	7113	Patto	7149

Paul	7150	Peni	7193
Pauld	7151	Penn	7194
Pauli	7152	Penne	7195
Paull	7153	Penni	7196
Paulsen	7154	Penno	7197
Pauly	7155	Penny	7198
Pav	7156	Peno	7199
Paw	7157	Pent	7200
Pax	7158	Peo	7201
Pay	7159	Pep	7202
Payn	7160	Pepp	7203
Pays	7161	Per	7204
Pea	7162	Perc	7205
Peac	7163	Perd	7206
Peal	7164	Perf	7207
Pear	7165	Perh	7208
Pearl	7166	Perk	7209
Pears	7167	Perl	7210
Pearso	7168	Perli	7211
Peas	7169	Perlo	7212
Pec	7170	Pern	7213
Peck	7171	Pero	7214
Ped	7172	Perr	7215
Pee	7173	Perri	7216
Peek	7174	Perro	7217
Peer	7175	Perry	7218
Peet	7176	Pers	7219
Pef	7177	Pert	7220
Peh	7178	Pes	7221
Pei	7179	Pete	7222
Peir	7180	Peters	7223
Peis	7181	Petersen	7224
Pek	7182	Peterson	7225
Pel	7183	Peti	7226
Pell	7184	Petr	7227
Pelli	7185	Petro	7228
Pelm	7186	Petry	7229
Pelt	7187	Pett	7230
Pelz	7188	Petti	7231
Pem	7189	Petty	7232
Pena	7190	Pen	7233
Pend	7191	Pey	7234
Pene	7192	Pf	7235

Pfe	7236	Pir	7279
Pfen	7237	Pis	7280
Pfi	7238	Pit	7281
Pfl	7239	Pitm	7282
Pfo	7240	Pitt	7283
Pfr	7241	Pitts	7284
Pah	7242	Pitz	7285
Phe	7243	Pla	7286
Phelp	7244	Plai	7287
Phi	7245	Plan	7288
Philb	7246	Plas	7289
Philip	7247	Plat	7290
Philips	7248	Platt	7291
Phillip	7249	Platz	7292
Philo	7250	Plau	7293
Phipp	7251	Plav	7294
Pho	7252	Ple	7295
Phr	7253	Ples	7296
Pia	7254	Pli	7297
Pic	7255	Plo	7298
Pick	7256	Plu	7299
Picki	7257	Plun	7300
Pico	7258	Ply	7301
Pid	7259	Pn	7302
Pie	7260	Po	7303
Pien	7261	Pod	7304
Pier	7262	Poe	7305
Piers	7263	Pog	7306
Piet	7264	Poh	7307
Pig	7265	Poi	7308
Pike	7266	Pok	7309
Pil	7267	Pol	7310
Pill	7268	Pole	7311
Pilo	7269	Poli	7312
Pim	7270	Polk	7313
Pin	7271	Poll	7314
Pine	7272	Pollo	7315
Pink	7273	Polo	7316
Pinn	7274	Pom	7317
Pino	7275	Pomm	7318
Pint	7276	Pon	7319
Pio	7277	Poo	7320
Pip	7278	Poon	7321

—Q—

—R—

Raut	7481	Rehn	7524
Rav	7482	Rei	7525
Raw	7483	Reich	7526
Rawl	7484	Reicher	7527
Raws	7485	Reichm	7528
Ray	7486	Reid	7529
Raym	7487	Reidy	7530
Rayne	7488	Reif	7531
Rayno	7489	Reig	7532
Rays	7490	Reil	7533
Re	7491	Reilly	7534
Read	7492	Reim	7535
Reade	7493	Reime	7536
Readi	7494	Rein	7537
Ready	7495	Reine	7538
Reag	7496	Reiner	7539
Real	7497	Reinhard	7540
Ream	7498	Reinhart	7541
Rear	7499	Reinhe	7542
Reas	7500	Reini	7543
Reb	7501	Reink	7544
Rec	7502	Reinl	7545
Reco	7503	Reino	7546
Red	7504	Reis	7547
Rede	7505	Reise	7548
Redf	7506	Reisi	7549
Redi	7507	Reiss	7550
Redl	7508	Reit	7551
Redm	7509	Reith	7552
Redo	7510	Reitm	7553
Ree	7511	Reitz	7554
Reed	7512	Reix	7555
Reede	7513	Rel	7556
Reedy	7514	Rell	7557
Rees	7515	Rem	7558
Reeve	7516	Remi	7559
Ref	7517	Reml	7560
Rega	7518	Rems	7561
Rege	7519	Ren	7562
Regg	7520	Rend	7563
Rego	7521	Rene	7564
Reh	7522	Renk	7565
Rehl	7523	Renn	7566

Rens	7567	Rick	7610
Rent	7568	Ricke	7611
Renw	7569	Rickert	7612
Renz	7570	Ricket	7613
Rep	7571	Rickl	7614
Repp	7572	Rid	7615
Req	7573	Ride	7616
Res	7574	Ridg	7617
Resi	7575	Ridi	7618
Reso	7576	Rie	7619
Rest	7577	Ried	7620
Ret	7578	Riedem	7621
Rett	7579	Riedi	7622
Reu	7580	Rief	7623
Reue	7581	Rieg	7624
Reul	7582	Rieh	7625
Reut	7583	Riel	7626
Rev	7584	Riem	7627
Revi	7585	Rien	7628
Rew	7586	Riep	7629
Rex	7587	Ries	7630
Rey	7588	Riese	7631
Reyl	7589	Riess	7632
Reyn	7590	Riet	7633
Rez	7591	Rif	7634
Rha	7592	Rig	7635
Rhe	7593	Rigg	7636
Rheinh	7594	Rign	7637
Rhin	7595	Rih	7638
Rho	7596	Rik	7639
Rhod	7597	Ril	7640
Rhof	7598	Rim	7641
Ri	7599	Rin	7642
Ric	7600	Rind	7643
Rice	7601	Rine	7644
Rich	7602	Ring	7645
Richa	7603	Ringe	7646
Richards	7604	Rini	7647
Richardson	7605	Rinn	7648
Riche	7606	Rio	7649
Riehm	7607	Rip	7650
Richo	7608	Ripp	7651
Richt	7609	Ris	7652

Rise	7653	Rodm	7696
Risl	7654	Rodn	7697
Riss	7655	Rodr	7698
Rit	7656	Rods	7699
Rite	7657	Roe	7700
Ritt	7658	Roeb	7701
Ritti	7659	Roec	7702
Ritz	7660	Roede	7703
Riv	7661	Roedi	7704
Rivers	7662	Roef	7705
Rives	7663	Roel	7706
Rivi	7664	Roem	7707
Rix	7665	Roen	7708
Riz	7666	Roes	7709
Roa	7667	Roet	7710
Road	7668	Rof	7711
Roar	7669	Rog	7712
Rob	7670	Roge	7713
Robbi	7671	Rogg	7714
Robe	7672	Rogo	7715
Roberts	7673	Roh	7716
Robertson	7674	Rohe	7717
Robes	7675	Rohl	7718
Robi	7676	Rohm	7719
Robin	7677	Rohr	7720
Robins	7678	Roi	7721
Robinson	7679	Rol	7722
Robis	7680	Rolf	7723
Robs	7681	Roll	7724
Roc	7682	Rolli	7725
Rochf	7683	Rollo	7726
Rock	7684	Rom	7727
Rocka	7685	Roman	7728
Rocke	7686	Romane	7729
Rockf	7687	Romb	7730
Rockw	7688	Rome	7731
Rockwood	7689	Romer	7732
Rod	7690	Romi	7733
Rode	7691	Romm	7734
Roden	7692	Ron	7735
Roder	7693	Ronn	7736
Rodg	7694	Rood	7737
Rodi	7695	Roof	7738

Rudi	7825	Runn	7848
Rudl	7826	Rup	7849
Rudo	7827	Rus	7850
Rue	7828	Ruse	7851
Rued	7829	Rush	7852
Rueh	7830	Rusk	7853
Ruep	7831	Russ	7854
Ruet	7832	Russi	7855
Ruff	7833	Russo	7856
Rug	7834	Rust	7857
Rugg	7835	Rut	7858
Ruggl	7836	Ruth	7859
Ruh	7837	Rutl	7860
Ruhl	7838	Rutt	7861
Rui	7839	Rutz	7862
Rul	7840	Ruz	7863
Rum	7841	Rya	7864
Rumm	7842	Ryb	7865
Rump	7843	Ryd	7866
Rumr	7844	Rye	7867
Run	7845	Ryf	7868
Rune	7846	Ryn	7869
Runk	7847	Rys	7870

—S—

Sa	7871	Saint B	7888
Sab	7872	Saint C	7889
Sabi	7873	Saint D & E	7890
Sac	7874	Saint F	7891
Sach	7875	Saint G	7892
Sack	7876	Saint H & I	7893
Sacket	7877	Saint Ja	7894
Saco	7878	Saint John	7895
Sad	7879	Saint Jos	7896
Sae	7880	Saint La	7897
Saf	7881	Saint Lo	7898
Sag	7882	Saint M	7899
Sager	7883	Saint N	7900
Sah	7884	Saint Pat	7901
Sail	7885	Saint Paul	7902
Sailor	7886	Saint Peter	7903
Saint A	7887	Saint R	7904

Saint S	7905	Saro	7948
Saint T	7906	Sart	7949
Saint U	7907	Sas	7950
Saints	7908	Sat	7951
Sak	7909	Sau	7952
Sala	7910	Saul	7953
Sale	7911	Saun	7954
Sali	7912	Saur	7955
Sall	7913	Sauv	7956
Salm	7914	Sav	7957
Salo	7915	Saval	7958
Salp	7916	Savi	7959
Salt	7917	Savo	7960
Salv	7918	Saw	7961
Salz	7919	Sawy	7962
Sam	7920	Sax	7963
Samm	7921	Saxo	7964
Samo	7922	Say	7965
Samp	7923	Sayl	7966
Samps	7924	Sayr	7967
Sams	7925	Sb	7968
Samu	7926	Sea	7969
San	7927	Scan	7970
Sanb	7928	Scanlon	7971
Sanc	7929	Scann	7972
Sand	7930	Scar	7973
Sande	7931	Scari	7974
Sanders	7932	Sce	7975
Sanderson	7933	Scha	7976
Sandg	7934	Schac	7977
Sandl	7935	Schaeffer	7978
Sando	7936	Schaeg	7979
Sands	7937	Schaf	7980
Sane	7938	Schaff	7981
Sang	7939	Schag	7982
Sani	7940	Schal	7983
Sant	7941	Scham	7984
Sanu	7942	Schan	7985
Sap	7943	Schap	7986
Sapo	7944	Schapp	7987
Sar	7945	Schar	7988
Sarg	7946	Scharf	7989
Sari	7947	Scharm	7990

Scharp	7991	Schio	8034
Schat	7992	Schir	8035
Schau	7993	Schl	8036
Schaum	7994	Schlam	8037
Schav	7995	Schlan	8038
Sche	7996	Schle	8039
Schee	7997	Schleg	8040
Scheer	7998	Schlei	8041
Schef	7999	Schlem	8042
Schei	8000	Schles	8043
Scheid	8001	Schley	8044
Schein	8002	Schli	8045
Scheir	8003	Schlie	8046
Schel	8004	Schlim	8047
Schell	8005	Schlis	8048
Schelli	8006	Schlo	8049
Schem	8007	Schlos	8050
Schen	8008	Schlot	8051
Schep	8009	Schlu	8052
Scher	8010	Schlun	8053
Schere	8011	Schm	8054
Scherf	8012	Schme	8055
Scherm	8013	Schmel	8056
Schern	8014	Schmi	8057
Scherr	8015	Schmidt	8058
Sches	8016	Schmie	8059
Scheu	8017	Schmit	8060
Scheur	8018	Schmo	8061
Schey	8019	Schmu	8062
Schi	8020	Schn	8063
Schie	8021	Schnai	8064
Schiele	8022	Schnap	8065
Schier	8023	Schnau	8066
Schif	8024	Schne	8067
Schiffm	8025	Schnei	8068
Schil	8026	Schnel	8069
Schill	8027	Schni	8070
Schille	8028	Schno	8071
Schilli	8029	Schnu	8072
Schillo	8030	Scho	8073
Schim	8031	Schoe	8074
Schin	8032	Schoen	8075
Schine	8033	Schoenf	8076

Schoens	8077	Schup	8120
Schoep	8078	Schur	8121
Schoer	8079	Schus	8122
Schof	8080	Schust	8123
Schol	8081	Schut	8124
Scholl	8082	Schuy	8125
Schom	8083	Schwa	8126
Schon	8084	Schwabe	8127
Schone	8085	Schwai	8128
Schoo	8086	Schwal	8129
School	8087	Schwam	8130
Schoon	8088	Schwan	8131
Schop	8089	Schwar	8132
Schor	8090	Schwartz	8133
Schorr	8091	Schwartze	8134
Schot	8092	Schwarz	8135
Schou	8093	Schwarze	8136
Schra	8094	Schwarzm	8137
Schral	8095	Schwe	8138
Schram	8096	Schwei	8139
Schran	8097	Schweit	8140
Schre	8098	Schwel	8141
Schrem	8099	Schwer	8142
Schri	8100	Schwi	8143
Schrod	8101	Schwin	8144
Schroe	8102	Schwo	8145
Schrof	8103	Sci	8146
Schru	8104	Sco	8147
Schu	8105	Scof	8148
Schub	8106	Scog	8149
Schuc	8107	Scot	8150
Schuck	8108	Scott	8151
Schue	8109	Scov	8152
Schues	8110	Sera	8153
Schuf	8111	Scri	8154
Schul	8112	Scrim	8155
Schulm	8113	Scro	8156
Schult	8114	Scud	8157
Schultze	8115	Scul	8158
Schulz	8116	Sea	8159
Schulze	8117	Seal	8160
Schum	8118	Seam	8161
Schun	8119	Sear	8162

Sheaf	8249	Shoo	8292
Shear	8250	Shop	8293
Sheb	8251	Shor	8294
Shed	8252	Short	8295
Shee	8253	Shos	8296
Sheel	8254	Shot	8297
Sheer	8255	Shou	8298
Shef	8256	Shra	8299
Shei	8257	Shre	8300
Shein	8258	Shri	8301
Shel	8259	Shro	8302
Shell	8260	Shu	8303
Shelt	8261	Shul	8304
Shem	8262	Shult	8305
Shen	8263	Shum	8306
Shepa	8264	Shur	8307
Shepha	8265	Shus	8308
Shephe	8266	Shut	8309
Shepp	8267	Shw	8310
Sher	8268	Sia	8311
Sheri	8269	Sib	8312
Sherl	8270	Sic	8313
Sherm	8271	Sico	8314
Sherr	8272	Sid	8315
Sherw	8273	Sie	8316
Shet	8274	Sieber	8317
Shew	8275	Siebo	8318
Shi	8276	Sied	8319
Shiel	8277	Sieg	8320
Shiels	8278	Siegf	8321
Shif	8279	Siegl	8322
Shil	8280	Siegm	8323
Shim	8281	Siegr	8324
Shin	8282	Siek	8325
Shinn	8283	Siel	8326
Ship	8284	Siem	8327
Shir	8285	Sien	8328
Shirr	8286	Sier	8329
Shm	8287	Sies	8330
Sho	8288	Siev	8331
Shoe	8289	Sif	8332
Shok	8290	Sig	8333
Shon	8291	Sigl	8334

Slom	8421	Soi	8464
Slos	8422	Sok	8465
Slot	8423	Sol	8466
Slow	8424	Sole	8467
Slu	8425	Soli	8468
Sly	8426	Soll	8469
Small	8427	Solm	8470
Smalls	8428	Solo	8471
Smar	8429	Solt	8472
Smea	8430	Som	8473
Smee	8431	Somers	8474
Smi	8432	Somm	8475
Smil	8433	Sommers	8476
Smith	8434	Son	8477
Smithe	8435	Sone	8478
Smiths	8436	Soni	8479
Smo	8437	Sonn	8480
Smu	8438	Sonne	8481
Smy	8439	Sono	8482
Smythe	8440	Sont	8483
Sna	8441	Soo	8484
Sne	8442	Sop	8485
Snee	8443	Sor	8486
Snei	8444	Sorg	8487
Snel	8445	Sori	8488
Sneu	8446	Sorm	8489
Sni	8447	Sorr	8490
Snif	8448	Sos	8491
Snit	8449	Sot	8492
Sno	8450	Sou	8493
Snow	8451	Soun	8494
Snowd	8452	South	8495
Snu	8453	Southe	8496
Snyder	8454	Southg	8497
Soa	8455	Southwa	8498
Sobi	8456	Southwo	8499
Sobo	8457	Sonv	8500
Soc	8458	Sow	8501
Society	8459	Soy	8502
Sod	8460	Spa	8503
Soe	8461	Spae	8504
Sof	8462	Spah	8505
Soh	8463	Spai	8506

Spy	8593	Stapp	8636
Squ	8594	Star	8637
Squi	8595	Starb	8638
Squire	8596	Starf	8639
Sra	8597	Stari	8640
Sro	8598	Stark	8641
Sta	8599	Starl	8642
Staat	8600	Starr	8643
Stab	8601	Starra	8644
Stac	8602	Starrs	8645
Stack	8603	Stas	8646
Staco	8604	State	8647
Stad	8605	Staten	8648
Stadt	8606	Stati	8649
Stae	8607	Stau	8650
Staf	8608	Staud	8651
Stafford	8609	Stauf	8652
Stag	8610	Staup	8653
Stagg	8611	Stav	8654
Stah	8612	Stay	8655
Stai	8613	Ste	8656
Stain	8614	Stearns	8657
Stak	8615	Steb	8658
Stal	8616	Stec	8659
Stall	8617	Steck	8660
Stalo	8618	Steckl	8661
Stam	8619	Sted	8662
Stamf	8620	Stee	8663
Stamm	8621	Steel	8664
Stamp	8622	Steele	8665
Stan	8623	Steen	8666
Stand	8624	Steene	8667
Stande	8625	Steer	8668
Standi	8626	Stef	8669
Stanf	8627	Steffe	8670
Stang	8628	Steg	8671
Stani	8629	Stegm	8672
Stanl	8630	Steh	8673
Stann	8631	Stei	8674
Stans	8632	Steig	8675
Stanw	8633	Steil	8676
Stap	8634	Steim	8677
Stapleton	8635	Stein	8678

Steina	8679	Stert	8722
Steinbe	8680	Stet	8723
Steinbr	8681	Stett	8724
Steind	8682	Steu	8725
Steine	8683	Steue	8726
Steinert	8684	Steur	8727
Steinf	8685	Stev	8728
Steing	8686	Stevenson	8729
Steinh	8687	Stew	8730
Steini	8688	Stewart	8731
Steink	8689	Stey	8732
Steinl	8690	Sti	8733
Steinma	8691	Stickn	8734
Steinme	8692	Stid	8735
Steinmi	8693	Stie	8736
Steins	8694	Stief	8737
Steint	8695	Stieg	8738
Steinw	8696	Stieh	8739
Steir	8697	Stien	8740
Stel	8698	Stier	8741
Stelle	8699	Stif	8742
Stelli	8700	Stil	8743
Stellm	8701	Still	8744
Stellw	8702	Stillm	8745
Stelt	8703	Stills	8746
Stem	8704	Stim	8747
Stemp	8705	Stimp	8748
Sten	8706	Stine	8749
Steng	8707	Stiner	8750
Stenn	8708	Stinn	8751
Stent	8709	Stip	8752
Step	8710	Stir	8753
Stephe •	8711	Stit	8754
Stephenson	8712	Stiv	8755
Stepp	8713	Stix	8756
Ster	8714	Sto	8757
Sterl	8715	Stock	8758
Stern	8716	Stocki	8759
Sterna	8717	Stockt	8760
Sterne	8718	Stockw	8761
Sternf	8719	Stod	8762
Sterns	8720	Stoddart	8763
Sterr	8721	Stoe	8764

Stoeh	8765	Stras	8808
Stoep	8766	Strass	8809
Stoes	8767	Strat	8810
Stof	8768	Stratt	8811
Stog	8769	Strau	8812
Stoi	8770	Straus	8813
Stoke	8771	Straw	8814
Stol	8772	Stre	8815
Stoll	8773	Strec	8816
Stolm	8774	Stree	8817
Stolt	8775	Streete	8818
Stolz	8776	Streh	8819
Stom	8777	Strei	8820
Stone	8778	Streit	8821
Stoni	8779	Strel	8822
Stoo	8780	Strem	8823
Stop	8781	Stren	8824
Stor	8782	Stret	8825
Store	8783	Stri	8826
Storer	8784	Strickland	8827
Stori	8785	Strid	8828
Stork	8786	Strif	8829
Storm	8787	Strin	8830
Storr	8788	Strip	8831
Story	8789	Strit	8832
Storz	8790	Stro	8833
Stos	8791	Stroe	8834
Stot	8792	Stroh	8835
Stou	8793	Strohm	8836
Stout	8794	Strok	8837
Stov	8795	Strom	8838
Stow	8796	Strome	8839
Stowe	8797	Strong	8840
Str	8798	Stroo	8841
Strack	8799	Stros	8842
Strad	8800	Strou	8843
Strae	8801	Strous	8844
Strah	8802	Strout	8845
Strai	8803	Stru	8846
Strak	8804	Struck	8847
Stram	8805	Strue	8848
Stran	8806	Strul	8849
Strann	8807	Strus	8850

Strut	8851	Summers	8894
Stry	8852	Sumner	8895
Stu	8853	Sump	8896
Stub	8854	Sun	8897
Stuc	8855	Sund	8898
Stud	8856	Sundi	8899
Studi	8857	Sunn	8900
Studl	8858	Sup	8901
Stue	8859	Supp	8902
Stuer	8860	Sur	8903
Stug	8861	Suri	8904
Stui	8862	Surr	8905
Stul	8863	Surv	8906
Stum	8864	Sus	8907
Stump	8865	Suss	8908
Stun	8866	Sussi	8909
Stup	8867	Sut	8910
Stur	8868	Suti	8911
Sturgi	8869	Sutp	8912
Sturk	8870	Sutr	8913
Sturm	8871	Sutt	8914
Sturn	8872	Sutto	8915
Sturt	8873	Suv	8916
Sturz	8874	Suy	8917
Stut	8875	Sva	8918
Stutz	8876	Svo	8919
Stuy	8877	Swa	8920
Sty	8878	Swal	8921
Su	8879	Swam	8922
Suc	8880	Swan	8923
Sud	8881	Swans	8924
Sue	8882	Swant	8925
Suf	8883	Swar	8926
Sug	8884	Swartz	8927
Suge	8885	Swas	8928
Suh	8886	Sway	8929
Sui	8887	Swe	8930
Sul	8888	Sweet	8931
Sullivan	8889	Swen	8932
Sully	8890	Swep	8933
Sulz	8891	Swey	8934
Sulze	8892	Swi	8935
Sum	8893	Swift	8936

Swig	8937	Symp	8948
Swin	8938	Syms	8949
Swinn	8939	Syn	8950
Swis	8940	Syp	8951
Swit	8941	Syr	8952
Swo	8942	Syro	8953
Swords	8943	Sys	8954
Sy	8944	Sz	8955
Sykes	8945	Szi	8956
Syl	8946	Szo	8957
Sym	8947		

—T—

Ta	8958	Tea	8987
Tabo	8959	Teb	8988
Tac	8960	Tee	8989
Tad	8961	Tef	8990
Taf	8962	Tei	8991
Tag	8963	Tel	8992
Tagi	8964	Tell	8993
Tai	8965	Tem	8994
Tait	8966	Temp	8995
Tak	8967	Ten	8996
Tal	8968	Tene	8997
Tall	8969	Tenn	8998
Talo	8970	Tep	8999
Talm	8971	Ter	9000
Tam	8972	Terr	9001
Tan	8973	Terry	9002
Tann	8974	Terw	9003
Tanner	8975	Tes	9004
Tans	**8976**	Tess	9005
Tap	8977	Tet	9006
Tapper	8978	Teu	9007
Tar	8979	Tew	9008
Tari	8980	Tex	9009
Tarr	8981	Th	9010
Tas	8982	Thad	9011
Tat	8983	Thal	9012
Tau	8984	Thall	9013
Tav	8985	Tham	9014
Taylor	8986	That	9015

Thay	9016	Tid	9059
The	9017	Tie	9060
Thee	9018	Tiem	9061
Thei	9019	Tien	9062
Theis	9020	Tier	9063
Thel	9021	Tiet	9064
Them	9022	Tif	9065
Theo	9023	Tig	9066
Ther	9024	Tila	9067
Theu	9025	Tilf	9068
Thi	9026	Till	9069
Thie	9027	Tilli	9070
Thier	9028	Tillm	9071
Thies	9029	Tillo	9072
Thil	9030	Tilt	9073
Thim	9031	Tim	9074
Thir	9032	Time	9075
Tho	9033	Timm	9076
Thol	9034	Timo	9077
Thom	9035	Timp	9078
Thomas	9036	Tin	9079
Thome	9037	Tink	9080
Thomp	9038	Tinl	9081
Thoms	9039	Tins	9082
Thomson	9040	Tip	9083
Thon	9041	Tir	9084
Thor	9042	Tis	9085
Thorn	9043	Tisd	9086
Thornt	9044	Tisn	9087
Thorp	9045	Tit	9088
Thors	9046	Titt	9089
Thou	9047	Tiv	9090
Thra	9048	Tj	9091
Thro	9049	Toa	9092
Thru	9050	Tob	9093
Thu	9051	Tobi	9094
Thur	9052	Tobl	9095
Thurs	9053	Toc	9096
Thw	9054	Tod	9097
Thy	9055	Toe	9098
Tib	9056	Tof	9099
Tic	9057	Tog	9100
Tich	9058	Toi	9101

Tol	9102	Traf	9145
Toll	9103	Trag	9146
Tolm	9104	Trai	9147
Tom	9105	Trainor	9148
Tome	9106	Trait	9149
Toml	9107	Trak	9150
Tomps	9108	Tran	9151
Ton	9109	Trap	9152
Toni	9110	Trapp	9153
Tonn	9111	Tras	9154
Too	9112	Trat	9155
Took	9113	Trau	9156
Tool	9114	Traud	9157
Toomey	9115	Traut	9158
Toon	9116	Trav	9159
Top	9117	Traver	9160
Topl	9118	Travi	9161
Topp	9119	Tray	9162
Toppin	9120	Trea	9163
Tor	9121	Tread	9164
Tore	9122	Trean	9165
Tori	9123	Treas	9166
Torn	9124	Treat	9167
Torp	9125	Treb	9168
Torr	9126	Trec	9169
Torre	9127	Tree	9170
Torri	9128	Treg	**9171**
Tos	9129	Trei	9172
Toss	9130	Trel	9173
Tot	9131	Trem	9174
Tou	9132	Tremp	9175
Toum	9133	Tren	9176
Tous	9134	Treni	9177
Tov	9135	Trent	9178
Tow	9136	Trep	9179
Tower	9137	Tres	9180
Town	9138	Tret	9181
Towns	9139	Treu	9182
Toy	9140	Trev	9183
Tra	9141	Tri	9184
Trac	9142	Trie	9185
Trad	9143	Trif	9186
Trae	9144	Tril	9187

Trim	9188	Tuf	9223
Trin	9189	Tui	9224
Trio	9190	Tul	9225
Trip	9191	Tum	9226
Tripp	9192	Tun	9227
Tris	9193	Tuo	9228
Trit	9194	Tup	9229
Tro	9195	Tur	9230
Trog	9196	Turi	9231
Troj	9197	Turn	9232
Trol	9198	Turner	9233
Trom	9199	Turp	9234
Tron	9200	Turt	9235
Trop	9201	Tus	9236
Tros	9202	Tut	9237
Trot	9203	Tutt	9238
Trou	9204	Tuv	9239
Trow	9205	Twa	9240
Troy	9206	Twe	9241
Tru	9207	Twen	9242
True	9208	Twi	9243
Truh	9209	Twin	9244
Trum	9210	Two	9245
Trun	9211	Twy	9246
Trus	9212	Ty	9247
Trust	9213	Tyl	9248
Trut	9214	Tyn	9249
Try	9215	Tynb	9250
Ts	9216	Tynd	9251
Tub	9217	Tyne	9252
Tuc	9218	Tyng	9253
Tuck	9219	Typ	9254
Tucker	9220	Tyr	9255
Tud	9221	Tys	9256
Tue	9222	Tyt	9257

—U—

Ua	9258	Uh	9263
Ud	9259	Uhli	9264
Ue	9260	Ui	9265
Uf	9261	Ul	9266
Ug	9262	Ull	9267

Van No	9349	Vie	9392
Van Ol	9350	Vig	9393
Van Or	9351	Vil	9394
Van P	9352	Vin	9395
Van Ra	9353	Vine	9396
Van Ri	9354	Vins	9397
Van Sa	9355	Vio	9398
Van Si	9356	Vir	9399
Van T	9357	Vis	9400
Van Va	9358	Vit	9401
Van Vi	9359	Viv	9402
Van Wa	9360	Vl	9403
Van Wi	9361	Vo	9404
Van Wy	9362	Voel	9405
Van Z	9363	Vog	9406
Var	9364	Vogell	9407
Vark	9365	Vogt	9408
Vas	9366	Voh	9409
Vat	9367	Voi	9410
Vau	9368	Vol	9411
Vaughn	9369	Volk	9412
Vaus	9370	Volkm	9413
Vea	9371	Voll	9414
Ved	9372	Volm	9415
Vee	9373	Voln	9416
Veg	9374	Vom	9417
Vei	9375	Von	9418
Vel	9376	Von C	9419
Ven	9377	Von E	9420
Veni	9378	Von G	9421
Vera	9379	Von H	9422
Vere	9380	Von I	9423
Veri	9381	Von M	9424
Verm	9382	Von S	9425
Vern	9383	Voo	9426
Verr	9384	Vor	9427
Ves	9385	Vos	9428
Vet	9386	Vot	9429
Veu	9387	Vou	9430
Vi	9388	Vr	9431
Vick	9389	Vu	9432
Vict	9390	Vy	9433
Vid	9391		

Wie	9604	Wildn	9647
Wiec	9605	Wilds	9648
Wieck	9606	Wile	9649
Wied	9607	Wiles	9650
Wiede	9608	Wiley	9651
Wieder	9609	Wilh	9652
Wiedi	9610	Wilho	9653
Wieg	9611	Wili	9654
Wiegl	9612	Wilk	9655
Wieh	9613	Wilken	9656
Wiek	9614	Wilkens	9657
Wiel	9615	Wilkes	9658
Wiele	9616	Wilki	9659
Wiem	9617	Wilkins	9660
Wien	9618	Wilkinson	9661
Wiene	9619	Wilko	9662
Wienh	9620	Will	9663
Wier	9621	Willa	9664
Wies	9622	Willb	9665
Wiese	9623	Willc	9666
Wiesen	9624	Wille	9667
Wiesi	9625	Willen	9668
Wiesn	9626	Willer	9669
Wiet	9627	Willett	9670
Wig	9628	Willi	9671
Wigg	9629	Williams	9672
Wiggi	9630	Williamsb	9673
Wight	9631	Williamson	9674
Wightm	9632	Williard	9675
Wigl	9633	Willig	9676
Wil	9634	Willing	9677
Wilbi	9635	Willis	9678
Wilbu	9636	Willit	9679
Wilc	9637	Willm	9680
Wilcox	9638	Willn	9681
Wild	9639	Wills	9682
Wildb	9640	Willson	9683
Wilde	9641	Wiln	9684
Wilden	9642	Wilmo	9685
Wilder	9643	Wiln	9686
Wildes	9644	Wils	9687
Wildf	9645	Wilson	9688
Wildm	9646	Wilt	9689

Wiltm	9690	Witte	9733
Wim	9691	Wittem	9734
Win	9692	Witter	9735
Winant	9693	Witti	9736
Winc	9694	Wittig	9737
Wind	9695	Wittm	9738
Windi	9696	Wittn	9739
Windo	9697	Wittr	9740
Winds	9698	Witz	9741
Wine	9699	Wix	9742
Winer	9700	Wiz	9743
Wing	9701	Wl	9744
Wini	9702	Wo	9745
Wink	9703	Wod	9746
Winl	9704	Woe	9747
Winn	9705	Woel	9748
Winner	9706	Woer	9749
Wins	9707	Woes	9750
Winsl	9708	Wog	9751
Winso	9709	Woh	9752
Wint	9710	Wohlf	9753
Winterb	9711	Wohlg	9754
Winterd	9712	Wohlr	9755
Winters	9713	Wohn	9756
Wintersm	9714	Woj	9757
Wintj	9715	Wol	9758
Wip	9716	Wolc	9759
Wir	9717	Wold	9760
Wirt	9718	Wole	9761
Wis	9719	Wolf	9762
Wise	9720	Wolfe	9763
Wish	9721	Wolff	9764
Wisk	9722	Wolfs	9765
Wism	9723	Wolfson	9766
Wisn	9724	Woli	9767
Wiss	9725	Wolk	9768
Wissl	9726	Woll	9769
Wist	9727	Woller	9770
Wit	9728	Wollm	9771
With	9729	Wolln	9772
Witk	9730	Wolm	9773
Witm	9731	Wolp	9774
Witt	9732	Wols	9775

Wolt	9776	Wra	9818
Wolti	9777	Wray	9819
Wom	9778	Wre	9820
Won	9779	Wred	9821
Wood	9780	Wren	9822
Woodb	9781	Wrenn	9823
Woodc	9782	Wri	9824
Woode	9783	Wright	9825
Woodf	9784	Wrighti	9826
Woodg	9785	Wrigl	9827
Woodh	9786	Wro	9828
Woodi	9787	Wron	9829
Woodl	9788	Wrou	9830
Woodm	9789	Wu	9831
Woodn	9790	Wue	9832
Woodr	9791	Wues	9833
Woods	9792	Wuh	9834
Woodw	9793	Wui	9835
Woof	9794	Wul	9836
Woog	9795	Wull	9837
Wool	9796	Wun	9838
Woole	9797	Wunn	9839
Woolf	9798	Wuns	9840
Wooll	9799	Wup	9841
Wools	9800	Wur	9842
Woon	9801	Wurt	9843
Woos	9802	Wurz	9844
Wor	9803	Wus	9845
Word	9804	Wut	9846
Wore	9805	Wy	9847
Work	9806	Wyat	9848
Workm	9807	Wyb	9849
Worl	9808	Wyc	9850
World	9809	Wyg	9851
Worm	9810	Wyl	9852
Worn	9811	Wyll	9853
Worr	9812	Wym	9854
Worth	9813	Wyn	9855
Wortm	9814	Wynn	9856
Wot	9815	Wyo	9857
Wou	9816	Wys	9858
Woy	9817	Wyt	9859

—X—

—Y—

—Z—

Ze	9930	Zin	9965
Zec	9931	Zinn	9966
Zee	9932	Zins	9967
Zeh	9933	Zio	9968
Zei	9934	Zip	9969
Zeig	9935	Zipp	9970
Zeil	9936	Zir	9971
Zeis	9937	Zit	9972
Zeiss	9938	Zitt	9973
Zek	9939	Ziu	9974
Zel	9940	Zo	9975
Zell	9941	Zoc	9976
Zelt	9942	Zog	9977
Zem	9943	Zol	9978
Zen	9944	Zom	9979
Zenn	9945	Zoo	9980
Zent	9946	Zor	9981
Zep	9947	Zot	9982
Zer	9948	Zr	9983
Zere	9949	Zs	9984
Zero	9950	Zu	9985
Zet	9951	Zuc	9986
Zeu	9952	Zuck	9987
Zev	9953	Zud	9988
Zi	9954	Zug	9989
Zie	9955	Zuk	9990
Ziegler	9956	Zuna	9991
Zier	9957	Zup	9992
Zies	9958	Zus	9993
Zig	9959	Zuv	9994
Zil	9960	Zw	9995
Zilm	9961	Zwe	9996
Zim	9962	Zwi	9997
Zimm	9963	Zwil	9998
Zimmerm	9964	Zwir	9999

INDEX

—A—

Abbeys, Fa2.
Abbreviations, Ek2.
Abdomen, Ma1.
Aberration, Mental, M6.
Abnaki Indians, Hu1.
Abolitionists, S6.
Aborigines, N2.
Abscess, Surgery, Ms.
Absolution, T8.
Abstinence, M7.
Abyssinia, History, Ho4.
Academies, E1.
Accent, Ek4.
Accidence, Ek4.
Accident Insurance, C9.
Accidents, M8.
Accompaniment, Music, Fm2.
Accounts, Eb2.
Accumulators, Pe4.
Acetylene, Chemistry, Pc6.
Acetylene, Lighting, Uf.
Acids, Pe9.
Acoustics, P4.
Acoustics, Musical, Fm1.
Acrobats, Fs2.
Acrostics, Fs4.
Acting, Lp1.
Acting, Amateur, Lp4.
Actions at Law, Jt.
Actors, Biography, B.
Actresses, Biography, B.
Acts of the Apostles, Bible, T2.
Adages, La.
Addresses, Collections, Lo6.
Addresses, Individual, Lo5.

Adirondack Mountains, History, Hu9.
Administration, Business, Ec1.
Administrators and Executors, Js.
Admirals' Lives, B.
Admiralty, Hb7.
Adolescence, Mg.
Adoption, Law, Jp.
Adulteration, Chemical, Pc.
Adulteration, Foods, Mf1.
Adultery, Jt.
Adventists, Tc7.
Adventure, V9.
Adventurers' Lives, B.
Adversity, S4.
Advertising, Business, Eb.
Advertising, Illustration, Fd2.
Advertising, Typography, Fd8.
Advice to Men, Medical, Mg8.
Advice to Women, Medical, Mg3.
Aerial Navigation,P9.
Aerolites, Na.
Aerography, Ng7.
Aeronautics, P9.
Aeroplane, P9.
Aesthetics, F1.
Aesthetics, Music, Fm.
Affidavits, Jp.
Afghanistan, History, Hc5.
Africa History, British East, Ho4.
Africa History, Central, Ho5.
Africa History, Eastern, Ho4.
Africa History, General, Ho2.
Africa History, Northern, Ho3.
Africa History, Southern, Ho7.

Africa History, Western, Ho6.

Africa, Voyages and Travels, Central, Vo5.

Africa, Voyages and Travels, Eastern, Vo4.

Africa, Voyages and Travels, General, Vo2.

Africa, Voyages and Travels, Northern, Vo3.

Africa, Voyages and Travels, Southern, Vo7.

Africa, Voyages and Travels, Western, Vo6.

Age, Old, Mh2.

Agnosticism, Tc1.

Agreements, Building, Ub.

Agreements, Law, Js.

Agriculture, A.

Agriculture, Chemistry, Af1.

Agriculture, Education, A.

Agriculture, Fairs, A1.

Agriculture, Implements, A2.

Agriculture, Pests, Af8.

Aids to the Injured, M8.

Ainu, History, Hc1.

Air, Analysis, Pc5.

Air Brake, Ue7.

Air Engine, Ue3.

Air, Hygiene, Mh1.

Air, Liquid, P5.

Air, Meteorology, Ng7.

Air, Physics, P5.

Airplane, P9.

Air Pump, P4.

Airships, P9.

Alabama, U.S., Hu9.

Alaska, U.S., Ha3.

Albania, History, Ho.

Albany, New York U. S., Hu9.

Alberta, Canada, Ha2.

Albigenses, Tc6.

Alchemy, Pc1.

Alcohol, M7.

Alcoran, Tn3.

Ales, Db2.

Algae, Nh6.

Algebra, Pm3.

Algeria, History, Ho3.

Algeria, Voyages and Travels, Vo3.

Algonkian Indians, Hu1.

Aliens, Law, Jn.

Aliens, Naturalization, Se3.

Alkalies, Pc5.

Allegiance, Jn.

Allegories, La.

Allopathy, M3.

Alloys, Um.

Almanacs, Gr1.

Almsgiving, S4.

Almhouses, S4.

Alphabets, Language, Ek.

Alphabets, Lettering, F9d.

Alphabets, Ornamental, Fd9.

Alpine Plants, Nh1.

Alps, Mountains, History, Hf8.

Alsace-Lorraine, History, Hf6.

Altars, T9.

Alternating Currents, Pc2.

Aluminum, Uc9.

Aluminum Manufacture, Um1.

Alwar, History, Hc5.

Amalgamation, Ue9.

Amateur Operas, Fm4.

Amateur Theatricals, Lp4.

Amazon River, Ha8.

Amazons, History, H8.

Ambassadors, Law, Jn.

Ambassadors, Political Science, Sp.

Ambonde, History, Ho7.

Ambulances, M8.

America, History, Ha.

America, Voyages and Travels, Va.

America, British, History, Ha2.

America, British, Voyages and Travels, Va2.

America, Central, History, Ha4.

America, Central, Voyages and Travels, Va4.

America, North, Indians, History, Hu1.

America, North, Voyages and Travels, Va1.

America, South, History, Ha8.

America, South, Voyages and Travels, Va8.

America, United States, Government, Sp3.

America, United States, History, Hu3.

America, United States, Voyages and Travels, Vu.

American Aborigines, Hu1.

American Literature, L4.

American Party, Sp2.

American Revolution, Hu4.

Americanisms, Ek4.

Ammunition, Cm1.

Amoor River, Hr.

Amorites, History, He.

Amos, Bible, T2.

Amphibia, Nh6.

Amphitheatres, Fa.

Amputation, Ms.

Amulets, Ep9.

Amusements, Parlor, Fs3.

Amusements, Public, Fs2.

Ana, Literature, La.

Anabaptists, Tc6.

Anaesthetics, M3.

Anagrams, Lb8.

Analysis, Qualitative, Pc2.

Analysis, Quantitative, Pc3.

Analysis, Spectrum, Pc2.

Analytical Geometry, Pm4.

Analytical Mechanics, P4.

Anam, History, Hc4.

Anarchy, Se5.

Anatolia, History, Hc7.

Anatomy, Ma1.

Anatomy for Artists, Fd5.

Ancestry, Evolution, Mb.

Ancestry, Genealogy, Bc3.

Ancient Law, Ja.

Ancient Literature, L3.

Ancient World, H2.

Andalusia, History, Hs1.

Andes Mountains, History, Ha8.

Andorra, France, Hf1.

Anecdotes, Lb8.

Aneroid Barometer, P5.

Angelicans, Tc1.

Angels, T6.

Anger, Ep4.

Angling, Fs7.

Anglo-Saxon, History, Hb.

Anglo-Saxon, Literature, L4.

Angola, History, Hc7.

Aniline Colors, Chemistry, Pc9.

Aniline Colors, Manufacture, Um9.

Animal Electricity, Ep9.

Animal Food, Mf.

Animal Kingdom, Nh3.

Animal Locomotion, Nh3.

Animal Magnetism, Ep9.

Animal, Psychology, Nh3.

Animalcules, Nh4.

Animals, Domestic, A3.

Animals, Stories of, Nh9.

Animals, Trained, Circus, Fs2.

Animals, Wild, Nh3.

Animated Pictures, Fp4.

Annam, Asia, Hc4.

Annapolis, Maryland, U.S., Hu9.

Annealing, Um.

Annihilation, T6.

Annuals, Gr1.

Annuities, Pm2.

Annuities, Insurance, C6.

Anonyms, G2.

Antarctic Regions, Hn2.
Anthems, Fm5.
Anthology, Lp3.
Anthropology, Man, N.
Anthropology, Philosophy, Ep3.
Anthropometry, N.
Anti-Christ, T5.
Antidotes, M7.
Antigua, History, Ha6.
Antilles, Ha6.
Antiques, Collections, Fe9.
Antiquities, History, N.
Antiquities, Man, N2.
Antiquities, See Countries.
Antiseptics, M3.
Anti-Slavery, S6.
Antonyms, Ek4.
Ants, Nh4.
Apache Indians, Hu1.
Apes, Nh8.
Aphorisms, Lb8.
Apiary, Nh4.
Apiculture, A8.
Apocalypse, Bible, T3.
Apologetics, Tc.
Apoplexy, M3.
Apostles, Acts of, Bible, T2.
Apostles, Creed, T8.
Apostles, Lives, Br.
Apostolic Church, Tc.
Apothegms, La.
Apparatus, See Special Subjects.
Apparitions, Ep9.
Appendicitis, M3.
Appenzell, History, Hf9.
Apples, Ag4.
Applied Chemistry, Pc.
Applied Christianity, T9.
Applied Electricity, Pe.
Applied Thermodynamics, P3.
Apprentices, Political Economy, Se4.
Apprentices, Useful Arts, Ut.

Apulia, History, Hi1.
Aquarium, Nh6.
Aqueducts, Ue8.
Aquitania, History, H8.
Arabesque, Ornament, Fd4.
Arabia, History, Hc7
Arabs, History, Hc7.
Arameans, History, Hc7.
Ararat Mountains, Hc3.
Araucanian Indians, Ha6.
Arbitration, Ethics, Ep5.
Arbitration, Industrial, Se4.
Arbitration, International, Jn.
Arbor Day, Af9.
Arboriculture, Ag7.
Arbors, Ag7.
Arc-Lamps, Pe6.
Arc-Welding, Um1.
Archaeology, History, N.
Archaeology, Prehistoric, H7.
Archbishops, See Special Religions, Tc.
Archery, Fs8.
Arches, Architectural, Fd3.
Arches, Engineering, Ue6.
Architects, Biography, B.
Architectural Construction, Ub.
Architectural Drawing, Fd3.
Architectural Orders, Fa.
Architecture, Church, Fa2.
Architecture, Civil Fa3.
Architecture, Dictionaries, Fa.
Architecture, Domestic, Fa4.
Architecture, Essays, Fa.
Architecture, Gothic, Fa1.
Architecture, History, Fa9.
Architecture, Naval, Cn9.
Architecture, Roman, Fa1.
Architecture, Schools, Fa3.
Architecture, Theatres, Fa3.
Arctic Regions, History, Hn1.
Arctic Regions, Voyages and Travels, Vn1.

Ardennes, History, Hf.
Argentine, History, Ha8.
Argolis, History, Hk5.
Argonauts, Tn8.
Argot, Ek6.
Ariamism, Tn6.
Aristology, D2.
Arithmetic, Pm1.
Arizona, U.S., Hu9.
Arkansas, U.S., Hu9.
Armada, Spanish, Hs.
Armatures, Pe4.
Armenia, History, Hc7.
Arminianism, Tc6.
Armor, H8.
Armored Vessels, Naval, Cn9.
Armored Vessels, Shipbuilding, Cs.
Arms, Artificial, Ms6.
Arms, Heraldry, Bc2.
Arms, History, H7.
Arms, Hygiene, Mh7.
Arms, Surgery, Ms.
Arms and Armor, Manners and Customs, H8.
Arms and Armor, Military Science, Cm1.
Army, See Special Countries.
Arran, History, Hb4.
Arrest, Jt.
Arrow Heads, H8.
Arrows, Fs8.
Arsenals, Cm1.
Art, Anatomy, Fd5.
Art, Catalogues, F8.
Art, Crafts, Fd6.
Art, Education, F6.
Art, Essays, F4.
Art, Exhibitions, F8.
Art, Galleries, F8.
Art, History, F9.
Art, Metal Work, Fd6.
Art, Needlework, De.

Art, Teaching, E3.
Arteries, Ma1.
Artesian Wells, Ue8.
Artificial Flowers, Dc7.
Artillery, Cm1.
Artists, Biography, Collective, F3.
Artists, Biography, Individual, F2.
Artists, Works, F2.
Arts, Fine, F.
Arts, Fine, Essays, F4.
Arts, Fine, Historical, F9.
Arts, Fine, Legendary, F5.
Arts, Fine, Sacred, F5.
Arts, Useful, U.
Arts and Crafts, Fd6.
Aryans, Ethnology, N.
Aryans, History, H7.
Aryans, Language, Ek.
Asceticism, Tn6.
Ashanti, History, Ho5.
Asia, History, Hc9.
Asia, Voyages and Travels, Vc9.
Asia Minor, History, Hc7.
Asphalt, Ue6.
Assam, History, He5.
Assassination, Jt.
Assault, Jt.
Assaying, Ue9.
Assessment, Economy, Se2.
Assessment, Local, Sg1.
Assignments, Jp.
Assisi, History, H2.
Assurance, C9.
Assyria, History, Hc7.
Asteroids, Na.
Asthma, Me5.
Astrology, Ep9.
Astronomical Instruments, Na5.
Astronomy, Na.
Astronomy, Nautical, Na8.
Astrophysics, Na.
Asylum, Right of, J.

Asylums, M8.
Athabasca, History, Ha2.
Athanasian Creed, T8
Atheism, Tc1.
Athens, History, Hk5.
Athletics, Fs1.
Atlantic Cables, Pe8.
Atlantic Ocean, Ng9.
Atlases, Astronomy, N.
Atlases, Geography, V1.
Atmosphere, Ng7.
Atoms, Pc.
Atonement, T5.
Attica, History, Hk5.
Attorneys, Law, Jp.
Auckland Islands, History, Hc3.
Auction Bridge, Fs3.
Auctions, G1.
Auditing, Eb2.
Augustinians Tc2.
Auricular Confession, T8.
Aurora, Na.
Australia, History, Hc3.

Australia, Voyages and Travels, Vc3.
Australasia, History, Hc3.
Austria, History, Hg3.
Austria, Voyages and Travels, **Vg3.**
Authors' Books, Lb.
Authors' Criticisms, Lb3.
Authors' Lives B.
Authorship, Lb1.
Autographs, Lb5.
Automobile, Ut5.
Auto Suggestion, Ep2.
Autumn, Nh
Autumnal Catarrh, Me.
Ava, History, Hc4.
Avalanches, Ng2.
Avesta, Tn4.
Aviation, P9.
Azerbijan, Asia, Hc9.
Azores, History, Hs7.
Aztec Indians, Ha5.

—B—

Babylon, History, Hc7.
Babylon, Voyages and Travels, Vc7.
Backgammon, Fs3.
Bacon, Vs, Shakespeare, Ls4.
Bacteria, M2.
Baden, History, Hg.
Bagdad, History, Hc7.
Bahai, Religion, Tn4.
Bahamas, History, Ha6.
Bailments, Js.
Baireuth, History, Hg5.
Baking, D3.
Balata, Um5.
Baldness, Mh6.
Baleric Island, Hs7.
Balkans, History, Hg6.

Ball Playing, Fs1.
Ballads, Literature, Lp.
Ballads, Music, Fm3.
Ballads, Poetry, Lp3.
Ballet, Fs4.
Ballistics, Cm1.
Ballooning, P9.
Ballot, Sp.
Balls, Dancing, Fs4.
Balls, Ethics, Ep5.
Balsams, Um5.
Baltic, History, Hr2.
Baltimore, Maryland, U.S., Hu9.
Baluchistan, History, Hc5.
Bamboo Work, Fa6.
Banditti, Law, Jt.
Bandy, Hockey, Fs8.

Bangkok, History, Hc4.
Bank Notes, Se8.
Bankers, Biography, B.
Banking, Se8.
Bankruptcy, Jp.
Banks and Banking, Se8.
Banners, Bc9.
Baptism, T8.
Baptisteries, T9.
Baptists, Tc4.
Bar, J.
Barbados, History, Ha6.
Barbary States, History, Ho3.
Barbuda, History, Ha6.
Barcelona, History, Hs1.
Bards, See Poetry.
Barley, Af2.
Barns, Architecture, Fa4.
Baroda, History, Hc5.
Barometer, Ng7.
Baronage, Bc2.
Barrows, N.
Baruch, Bible, T2.
Baseball, Fs1.
Bashan, History, Hc7.
Basilicas, Fa2.
Basketry, D8.
Bas-relief, Fd7.
Bastile, History, Hf.
Basutoland, South Africa, Ho7.
Batavia, History, Hc3.
Bath, History, Hb1.
Baths, Mh4.
Batrachia, Nh6.
Bats, Nh8.
Batteries, Army, Cm1.
Batteries, Electric, Pe2.
Batteries, Navy, Cn1.
Battle, Wager of, J.
Battles, See Countries.
Bavaria, History, Hg5.
Bayonets, Cm1.
Bayreuth, History, Hg5.

Beaches, Ng.
Beacons, Cn6.
Beads, Church, T8.
Beadwork, Dc6.
Beams, Strength of, Ue6.
Bears, Stories, Nh9.
Bears, Zoology, Nh3.
Beasts, Nh3.
Beatitudes, T2.
Beautiful, The, F1.
Beauty, Art, F1.
Beauty, Hygiene, Nh3.
Beaver, Stories, Nh9.
Beaver, Zoology, Nh3.
Bechuanaland, History, Ho7.
Bedouins, History, Hc7.
Beds, Mh.
Bee-keeping, A8.
Beer, Brewing, Db2.
Beer, Analysis, Pc.
Beer, Temperance, M7.
Bees, Nh4.
Beetles, Nh4.
Beggars and Begging, S4.
Behavior, E7.
Being, Ep2.
Belgium, History, Hg8.
Belgium, Voyages and Travels,
   Vg8.
Belgium Congo, History, Ho5.
Belief, Philosophy, Ep2.
Belief, Theology, T6.
Belles, Lettres, L.
Bell Ringing, Fm8.
Bells, Church, T8.
Bells, Clock, Um2.
Bells, Electric, Pe7.
Belting, Ue1.
Beluchistan, History, Hc5.
Benedictines, Tc1.
Benefit of Clergy, Law, Ja.
Benevolence, Philosophy, Ep5.
Benevolence, Societies, S9.

Bengal, History, Hc5.
Bennington, Vermont, U.S., **Hu9.**
Beowulf, Lp2.
Berbers, History, Ho3.
Berkshire Mountains, Mass., U.S., Hu9.
Berlin, History, Hg1.
Bermuda, History, Ha6.
Bermuda, Voyages and Travels, Va6.
Betting, Ep4.
Beverages, Adulteration, **Mf1.**
Beverages, Manufacture, Db.
Beverages, Temperance, M7.
Bezique, Fs3.
Bhagavada Gita, Lp8.
Bible, T2.
Bible, Commentaries, T3.
Bible, Separate Books, T2.
Bible, Studies, Teaching, T2.
Bibliography, G2.
Bibliomania, G2.
Bicycling, Fs8.
Bilious Fever, Mf2.
Billiards, Fs3.
Bills of Credit, Js.
Bills of Exchange, Se8.
Bimetallism, Se7.
Binding, Ut7.
Biographical Dictionaries, Bc1.
Biography, Arts and Artists, Collectives, F3.
Biography, Arts and Artists, Individual, F2.
Biography, Collective, Bc.
Biography, Individual, B.
Biography, General, Bc1.
Biography, Religious, Br.
Biography, Shakespeare, Ls2.
Biology, Mb.
Biometry, C6.
Bioplasm, Mb.
Biplanes, P9.

Birds, Nh7.
Birthdays, H8.
Bishops, Lives, B.
Bison, Nh3.
Black Art, Ep9.
Black Death, Mh9.
Black Feet Indians, Hu1.
Black Forest, History, Hg1.
Black Hills, U.S., Hu9.
Black Sea, History, Hc7.
Blacksmithing, Ut4.
Blasphemy, Ethics, Ep5.
Blasphemy, Law, Jp.
Blasting, Engineering, Ue9.
Bleaching, Um9.
Bleeding, Surgery, Ms.
Bleeding, Therapeutics, M3.
Blind, Education of, E3.
Blindness, Me2.
Block-books, G9.
Block Island, Rhode Island, U.S., Hu9.
Blockade, Law, Jn.
Blood, M.
Bloodletting, M3.
Blowpipe, Pc3.
Blue Law, J.
Blue Print, Reading, Fd3.
Blue Print, Printing, Fp.
Blunders, Etiquette, E7.
Blunders, Language, See **Countries.**
Boat Building, Cs.
Boating, Fs6.
Body, Care of, Mh4.
Body, Human, Ma1.
Body and Mind, Ep3.
Boers, History, Ho7.
Boeotia, History, Hk5.
Bogota, History, Ha8.
Bohemia, History, Hg4.
Bohemia, Language, Ek9.
Bohemia, Literature, L9.

Boilers, Ue5.
Boilers, Insurance, C9.
Bokhara, History, Hc5.
Bolivia, History, Ha6.
Bolsheviki, Se5.
Bombay, History, Hc5.
Bonds, Se8.
Bones, Animal, Nh3.
Bones, Disease, M3.
Bones, Human, Ma1.
Bones, Paleontology, Ng3.
Bones, Physiology, Ma2.
Book Clubs, E5.
Book Illustration, Fd2.
Book of Fate, Ep9.
Bookbinding, Ut7.
Bookkeeping, Eb2.
Bookplates, Lb9.
Books and Reading, Lb.
Books, Bibliography, G2.
Books, Collections, G9.
Booksellers Catalogues, G1.
Book Selling, Eb7.
Boot Making, Ut6.
Boots, Clothing, Dc.
Bordeaux, History, Hf1.
Boring, Ue8.
Borneo, History, Hc3.
Boroughs, Sg.
Bosnia, History, Hg4.
Bosphorus, History, Vc7.
Boston, Massachusetts, U.S., Hu9.
Boston, Tea Party, Hu4.
Botanists, Lives, B.
Botany, Nh1.
Boulders, Ng1.
Boundaries, Law, Jn.
Bounty, Ship, Mutiny of, Hc2.
Bow, Musical, Fm8.
Bowling, Fs3.
Boxing, Fs1.
Boycotting, Se4.
Brahminism, Tn1.

Brain, Anatomy, Ma1.
Brain, Diseases, M5.
Brain, Mental Philosophy, Ep3.
Brain, Physiology, Ma2.
Brakes, Air, Ue7.
Brakes, Electric, Pe5.
Brandy, Ethics, M7.
Brandy, Manufacture, Db.
Brass, Arts and Crafts, Fd6.
Brass Manufacture, Um2.
Brass, Sculpture, Fd7.
Brasses, T8.
Bravery, Ep5.
Brazil, History, Ha6.
Bread, Adulteration, Mf.
Bread, Manufacture, D3.
Breakwater, Ue6.
Breast, Ma1.
Breath, Disease, Mf2.
Breathing, Musical, Fm7.
Breathing, Physical Culture, Me2.
Breeding, Agriculture, A.
Breeding, Animals, Cattle, A4.
Breeding, Horses, A6.
Brewing, Db.
Bric-a-brac, Fd6.
Bric-a-brac, Antiques, Fe9.
Bricks, Ub1.
Bridge, Whist, Fs3.
Bridges, Ue6.
Brigands, Law, Jt.
Brighton, England, Hb1.
Bristol, England, Hb1.
Bristol, Massachusetts, U.S. Hu9.
British America, History, Ha2.
British Constitution, Sp4.
British Columbia, History, Ha2.
British East Africa, History, Ho4.
British Guiana, History, Ha8.
British Honduras, History, Ha4.
British Parliament, Sp4.
British Somaliland, History, Ho3.
Brittany, History, Hf1.

Broadcasting, Radio, Pe8.
Brokers, Biography, B.
Bronchitis, Me5.
Bronx, New York, U.S. Hu9.
Bronze, Age, H7
Bronze, Manufactures, Um2.
Bronzes, Fd7.
Bronzing, Um2.
Brooklyn, New York, U.S. Hu9.
Broom Making, D8.
Brotherhoods, See Religions.
Brownists, Tc6.
Brunei, History, IIc3.
Bruises, M8.
Brush-making, D8.
Brussels, History, Hg8.
Brutes, Nh3.
Bryology, Nh1.
Buccaneers, V6.
Bucolic Poetry, Lp2.
Budapest, History, Hg3.
Buddhism, Tn1.
Buds, Botany, Nh1.
Buds, Gardening, Ag.
Buffalo, New York, U.S. Hu9.
Building, Ub.
Building, Associations, Se9.
Building, Concrete, Uc2.
Building, Estimates, Ub.
Building, Inspection, Sg2.
Building, Laws, Js.
Building, Materials, Uc1-2.
Building, Plans and Specifications, Ub.

Building, Steel Construction, Ue2.
Bulbs, Ag5.
Bulgaria, History, Hb6.
Bull Fights, Fs1.
Bullion, Se7.
Bungalows, Fa4.
Bunker Hill, Massachusetts, U.S. Hu4.
Burglary, Jt.
Burgundy, History, Hf1.
Burial, Customs, H8.
Burial, Hygiene, Mh9.
Burial Service, See Special Religions.
Burmah, History, Hc4.
Burning the Dead, Mh9.
Burns and Scalds, M8.
Burying Grounds, Ag9.
Business, Eb.
Business, Administration, Eb1.
Business, Correspondence, Eb4.
Business, History, Eb9.
Business, Law, Jp.
Business, Management, Eb1.
Business, Writing, Eb4.
Butter, Adulteration, Mf1.
Butter, Chemistry, Pc2.
Butter, Dairy, A5.
Butterflies, Nh4.
Byzantine, Architecture, Fa1.
Byzantine, Empire, History, Hk5.
Byzantium, History, Ho.

—C—

Cabinet Work, Fa6.
Cabala, Ep1.
Cactus, Nh2.
Caffres (Kafirs), Ho7.
Cage Birds, Nh7.
Cairo, History, He.

Cairo, Voyages and Travels, Ve.
Calculating Machines, Pm.
Calculus, Pm3.
Calcutta, History, Hc5.
Calendar, Na9.
Calico, Printing, Um9.

California, U.S., Hu9.

Califs, Tn3.

Caliphs, Tn3.

Calisthenics, Mp.

Caloric, P3.

Calorimeter, P3.

Calvinism, Tc6.

Cambistry, Pm9.

Cambodia, History, Hc4.

Cameos, Fe3.

Camera, Fp.

Cameroons, Tc5.

Camp-meetings, Tc9.

Camping, Fs9.

Camps, Architecture, Fa5.

Camps, Hygiene, Mh1.

Cams, Ue3.

Canaan, History, Hc7.

Canada, History, Ha2.

Canada, Voyages and Travels, Va2.

Canal Zone, Panama, Ha8.

Canals, Commerce, C1.

Canals, Engineering, Ue8.

Canary Islands, History, Ha6.

Cancer, M3.

Candles, Um7.

Candlesticks, Fd6.

Candy, D5.

Cannibalism, H8.

Cannon, Cm1.

Canoe Building, Cs.

Canoeing, Fs6.

Canon Law, Ja.

Canonization, Tc1.

Cantatas, Books About, Fm6.

Cantatas, Music, Fm3.

Canterbury, England, Hb.

Canton, History, He.

Caoutchouc, Um5.

Cape Cod, Massachusetts, U.S. Hu9.

Cape Colony, History, Ho7.

Cape of Good Hope, History, Ho7.

Capital, Se4.

Capital Punishment, Jt.

Cap-making, Ut8.

Capuchins, Tc2.

Car-building, Ue7.

Car, Electric, Pe4.

Carbon, Pc6.

Carbon Printing, Fp4.

Cardinals, Lives, Br.

Cards, Ethics, Ep5.

Cards, Games, Fs3.

Cards, Tricks with, Fs5.

Caria, History, Hc9.

Caribbean Sea, Ha6.

Caribbee Islands, History, Ha6.

Caricature, Fd1.

Carlsbad, History, Hg1.

Carnations, Ag5.

Caroline Islands, History, Hc2.

Carols, Music, Fm5.

Carols, Poetry, Lp3.

Carpathian Mountains, Hg3.

Carpentry, Ub3.

Carpentry, Woodworking, Ub4.

Carpets, Furniture, D9.

Carpets, Manufacture, Um8.

Carriage, Painting, Ub6.

Carriages, Ut1.

Carriers, Commerce, C.

Carriers, Express, C2.

Carriers, Law, Jn.

Carriers, Railroads, C2.

Carriers, Shipping, C1.

Cars, Ue7.

Cartesian Philosophy, Ep2.

Carthage, History, Ho3.

Carthusians, Tc2.

Cartography, V1.

Cartoons, Fd2.

Carving, Fe3.

Cases of Conscience, Ep5.

Cashmere, History, Hc5.

C—Continued.

Caste, Philosophy, Ep5.
Caste, Sociology, S.
Castile, History, Hs1.
Casting, Ue2.
Castles, Fa4.
Casuistry, Ep5.
Cat, A3.
Catacombs, Ag9.
Cataloging, G3.
Catalogues, Private, G6.
Catalogues, Public, G5.
Catalonia, History, Hs7.
Cataracts, Eye, Me2.
Cataracts, Physical Geography, Ng9.
Catarrh, Me5.
Catechisms, T8.
Catering, D3.
Caterpillars, Nh4.
Cathedrals, Fa2.
Cathode Rays, Pe6.
Catholic Church, Tc2.
Catskill Mountains, New York, U.S. Hu9.
Cattle, A4.
Caucasus, History, Hr2.
Caucus, Sp.
Cavalry, Cm2.
Caves, Archaeology, N.
Caves, Geology, Ng8.
Cayari River, Ha6.
Celebes, History, Hc3.
Celestial Scenery, Na.
Celibacy, Mg6.
Celibacy, Philosophy, Ep5.
Cell, Voltaic, Pe2.
Cello, Fm8.
Cells, Biology, Mb.
Celluloid, Manufacture, Um5.
Cellulose, Um5.
Celtic Poetry, Lp3.
Cement, Ub2.
Cemeteries, Ag9.

Cemeteries, Hygiene, Mh9.
Censorship of the Press, Sp.
Census, S2.
Centennial Exhibitions, U.
Central Africa, History, Ho5.
Central America, History, Ha4.
Central America, Voyages and Travels, Va4.
Ceramics, Fine Arts, Fe.
Ceramics, Manufacturers, Um4.
Cereals, Af2.
Ceremonies, Manners and Customs, H8.
Ceremonies, Religious, T8.
Certainty, Ep2.
Cévennes Mountains, Hf.
Ceylon, History, Hc5.
Ceylon, Voyages and Travels, Vc5.
Chafing Dish, D6.
Chained Books, Lb.
Chains, Um1.
Chair Caning, D8.
Chairs, Fa6.
Chaldea, History, Hc7.
Champagne, France, Hf1.
Champlain, Lake, U.S. Hu9.
Chance, Amusement, Fs4.
Chance, Gambling, Ep4.
Chancellors, Lord, B.
Chancery, Court, Jt.
Chancery, Law, Jp.
Chanting, Fm5.
Chants, Fm5.
Chap-books, G9.
Chapels, Fa2.
Character, Ep6.
Charades, Acting, Lp4.
Charades, Amusement, Fs4.
Charcoal, Chemistry, Pc9.
Charcoal, Fuel, Uf.
Charcoal Drawing, Fd2.
Chariots, H8.
Charitable Societies, S9.

140

Charities, S4.

Charity, Ethics, Ep6.

Charity, Sociology, S4.

Charity Schools, Tc9.

Charleston, So. Carolina, U.S. Hu9.

Charlestown, Massachusetts, U.S. Hu9.

Chartres, France, Hf1.

Chartreuse, France, Hf1.

Charts, V1.

Charts, Graphic, Fd3.

Chase, Fs9.

Chastity, Ep5.

Chateaux, Fa4.

Chatham Islands, Hc3.

Chattels, Jp.

Cheating, Ep5.

Checkers, Fs3.

Cheese, A5.

Cheirosophy, Ep7.

Chemistry, Pc.

Chemistry, Analytical, Pc2.

Chemistry, Calculations, Pc.

Chemistry, Experiments, Pc4.

Chemistry, Industrial, Pc9.

Chemistry, Inorganic, Pc5.

Chemistry, Medical, Pc7.

Chemistry, Organic, Pc6.

Chemistry, Photography, Fp3.

Chemistry, Physiological, Pc7.

Chemistry, Quantitative, Pc3.

Chemistry, Technology, Pc9.

Chesbourg, History, Hf1.

Cheshire, England, Hb1.

Chess, Fs3.

Chest, Anatomy, Ma1.

Chest, Diseases, Me5.

Chest, Operations, Ms.

Chicago, Illinois, U.S. Hu9.

Chicken-pox, M3.

Chickens, A7.

Chief Justices, Lives, B.

Child Study, E3.

Children, Care, M8.

Children, Diseases, Mg4.

Children, Education, E3.

Children, Ethics, Ep6.

Children's Crusade, H3.

Children's Poetry, Lp4.

Chile, History, Ha6.

Chiming, Fm8.

Chimney Sweeping, Uf.

Chimneys, Ub1.

China, Fine Arts, Fc.

China, History, Hc.

China, Manufactures, Um4.

China, Painting, Fe1.

China, Voyages and Travels, Vc.

Chincha Islands, Ha8.

Chinese Language, Ek9.

Chinese Literature, L9.

Chinese Philosophy, Ep1.

Chinese Religion, Tn4.

Chippewa Indians, Hu1.

Chiromancy, Ep9.

Chitral, History, Ho5.

Chivalry, H3.

Chloroform, Drugs, M1.

Chloroform, Poisons, M7.

Chlorosis, M3.

Chocolate, D5.

Cholera, M3.

Choral Service, Fm5.

Christ, T5.

Christian Art and Symbolism, F5.

Christian Biography, Br.

Christian Doctrine, T4.

Christian Education, T8.

Christian Ethics, Ep5.

Christian Healing, Ep9.

Christian History, Tc.

Christian Life, T8.

Christian Science, Ep9.

Christian Union, Tc.

Christianity, Tc.

Christian, H8.
Christology, T5.
Chromatics, P2.
Chronicles, Bible, T2.
Chromolithography, Fe1.
Chronology, Astronomy, Na9.
Chronology, Bible, Tc.
Chronology, History, H6.
Chrysanthemum, Ag5.
Church, Tc.
Church and Sociology, S5.
Church and State, Philosophy, Ep5.
Church and State, Political Science, S4.
Church and State, Theology, Tc.
Church Architecture, Fa2.
Church Benefices, Tc.
Church Biography, Br.
Church Ceremonies, T8.
Church Costume, T8.
Church Decoration and Ornament, Fd4.
Church Dedication, T8.
Church Fathers, Biography, Br.
Church Festivals, T8.
Church Furniture, T8.
Church Government, T8.
Church History, Tc.
Church Law, Ja.
Church Membership, T8.
Church Music, Fm5.
Church of England, Tc3.
Church of Scotland, Tc5.
Church Polity, Tc.
Church Property, T8.
Church Rates, Tc.
Church Services, See Religions.
Church Unity, Tc.
Church Vestments, T8.
Churchyards, Ag9.
Cid, Chronicles of, Lp5.
Cinch, Cards, Fs3.

Cincinnati, Ohio, U.S. Hu9.
Cipher, Eb5.
Cipher, Telegraph, Pe8.
Circassia, History, Hr1.
Circles, Architecture, Fd5.
Circles, Geometry, Pm4.
Circulation of the Blood, Ma2.
Circumcision, Mg6.
Circumnavigation, V3.
Circular Curves, Pm6.
Circus, Fs2.
Cistercians, Tc1.
Cities, Government, Sg.
Cities, Hygiene, Mh1.
Cities, Sewage, Ub8.
Citizenship, Law, Jn.
City Planning, Sg4.
Civics, U.S. Sp3.
Civil Engineering, Ue6.
Civil Government, Sg.
Civil Law, Jp.
Civil Liberty, Se.
Civil Service, Administration, Sp.
Civil Service, Local Governments, Sg.
Civil Trials, Jt.
Civil War, U.S., Hu6.
Civilization, H7.
Clairvoyance, Ep9.
Clans, Sp.
Clans, Scottish, Hb4.
Classical Antiquities, N.
Classical Biography, B.
Classical Dictionaries, H5.
Classical Education, E4.
Classical Geography, V1.
Classical Literature, L7.
Classical Mythology, Tn5.
Classification, Library, G3.
Clay-modeling, Fd6.
Clays, Ng8.
Cleaning, Um9.
Cleanliness, Mh4.

Clearing House, Se8.
Clergy, Biography, Br.
Cleveland, Ohio, U.S. Hu9.
Cliff Dwellings, H7.
Climate, Ng7.
Climbing Plants, Nh1.
Clinical Medicine, M.
Clocks, Furniture, Fa6.
Clocks and Watches, Manufacturers, Ut3.
Close Communion, T8.
Cloth, Um8.
Clothing, Dc.
Clouds, Ng7.
Clubs, Social, S9.
Coaches, Ut1.
Coaching, Fs8.
Coaching, Transportation, C2.
Coal Fuel, Uf.
Coal Gas, Uf.
Coal Metallurgy, Ue9.
Coal, Mineralogy, Ng6.
Coal, Mining, Ue9.
Coal, Oil, Pc9.
Coal Tar, Colors, Pc9.
Coast Pilots, Cn5.
Coast Survey, Na7.
Coat of Arms, Bc2.
Cochin, China, Hc.
Cocoa, D4.
Co-education, E2.
Coffee, Agriculture, Af6.
Coffee, Domestic Science, D4.
Coffee, Stimulants, M7.
Coffer-dams, Ue8.
Coffins, H8.
Cog Wheels, Ue1.
Coils, Electric, Pc2.
Coinage, Se7.
Coins, Medals, Fe5.
Coke, Chemistry, Pc9.
Coke, Fuel, U8.
Colds, M3.

Coleoptera, Nh4.
Colic, M3.
Collected Biography, Bc.
Collections, Antiques, Fe9.
Colleges and Universities, E1.
Collisions, Law, Jn.
Colombia, History, Ha8.
Colon, Disease, M3.
Colonial America, Hu2.
Colonial Architecture, Fa4.
Colonial History, Hu2.
Colonies, Se3.
Colonization, Se3.
Color, Artists, Fd1.
Color-blindness, Me.
Color, Chemistry, Pc9.
Communism, Se5.
Community, Organizations, S9.
Commutators, Pe5.
Como Lake, Hi1.
Comparative Anatomy, Botany, Nh1.
Comparative Anatomy, Zoology, Nh3.
Comparative Literature, L3.
Compass, Cn5.
Compensations, Se4.
Competition, Se4.
Competitive Examinations, Civil Service, Sp.
Competitive Examinations, Local Governments, Sg.
Competitive Examinations, Schools, E3.
Complexion, Diseases, M4.
Complexion, Hygiene, Mh3.
Composers, Lives, B.
Composite Architecture, Fa.
Composite Photography, Fp4.
Composition, English, Ek2.
Composition, Musical, Fm1.
Composition, Pictorial, Fd2.
Composition, Printing, Fd8.

Compressed Air, Ue.

Compromise Law, International, Jn.

Compromise Law, Special, Js.

Compulsory Education, E1.

Concealed Tuberculosis, Me5.

Concerto, Score, Music, Fm4.

Conchology, Nh6.

Conciliation, Se4.

Concord, Massachusetts, U.S. Hu9.

Concord, Revolutionary War, Hu4.

Concordance, Bible, T4.

Concrete, Ub2.

Concrete Buildings, Fa4.

Concrete, Manufacture, Ub2.

Concrete, Materials, Ub2.

Condemned Books, G8.

Condensers, Chemical, Pc.

Condensers, Electric, Pe2.

Condensers, Steam, Ue5.

Condiments, D7.

Conduct of Life, Ep5.

Conduits, Electric, Pe8.

Conduits, Sanitation, Ue8.

Conduits, Telegraph, Pe8.

Conduits, Water, Ue8.

Confederate States, U.S. History, Hu6.

Confederation, U.S. Hu4.

Confederation, Germany, Hg.

Confectionery, D5.

Confession, T8.

Confirmation, T8.

Confiscation, J.

Conflagrations, Uf2.

Confucianism, Tn4.

Congo Free States, History, Ho5.

Congregationalism, Tc6.

Congress, U.S. Sp3.

Congress, Documents, Ru.

Conic Sections, Pm4.

Conjuring, Fs5.

Connecticut, U.S. Hu9.

Consanguinity, Jp.

Conscience, Ep5.

Consciousness, Ep5.

Conscription, Cm.

Consecration, T8.

Conservation of Energy, P6.

Conservatories, Music, Fm.

Conservatories, Plants, Nh.

Conspiracies, National, Jn.

Conspiracies, Trials, Jt.

Constables, Sg8.

Constantinople, History, Ho.

Constellations, Na2.

Constitution, England, Sp4.

Constitution, United States, Sp3.

Constitutional Law, Jc.

Construction, Architectural, Ue6.

Construction, Electric, Pe3.

Construction, Masonry, Ub.

Constructive Anatomy, Fd5.

Consumption, Me5.

Contagion, Mh9.

Contracts, Ethics, Ep5.

Contracts, Law, Js.

Contusions, M8.

Conundrums, Fs4.

Convents, Tc2.

Conversation, Ek3.

Conversation, Ethics, Ep4.

Conversion, Tc9.

Conveyancing, Js.

Convict Labor, Se6.

Convicts, Jt.

Cook Islands, History, Hc2.

Cookery, D3.

Cooking Schools, D3.

Co-operation, Banking, Se8.

Co-operation, Building and Loan Associations, Se9.

Co-operation, Labor, Se4.

Co-operative Associations, Se9.

Copenhagen, History, Hd1.

Copper, Engraving, Fe1.

Copper, Manufacturing, Um2.
Copper, Metallurgy, Ue9.
Copper, Money, Fe5.
Copper, Useful Arts, Um2.
Coypright, Law, Jn.
Coquetry, S7.
Coral Islands, Ng8.
Corals, Nh6.
Corea, History, Hc.
Corinthians, Bible, T2.
Corn, Af6.
Corn, Laws, Se.
Cornice-making, Um2.
Cornwall, England, Hb1.
Coronations, H8.
Coroners, Sg5.
Corporal Punishment, E3.
Corporations, Se1.
Corporations, Governments, Sg.
Corpulence, Mf.
Correlation of Forces, P6.
Correspondence, Business, Eb4.
Correspondence, Letter Writing, Ek2.
Corrosion, Pc.
Corsairs, V6.
Corsica, History, Hi2.
Cosmetics, Dc8.
Cosmogony, Creation, N.
Cosmogony, Metaphysics, Ep2.
Cosmography, Ng8.
Cosmology, Creation, N.
Cosmology, Metaphysics, Ep2.
Cossacks, History, Hr.
Cost, Accounting, Eb3.
Cost, Building, Ub.
Costa Rica, History, Ha4.
Costume, Design, Dc1.
Costume, Dress, Dc.
Costume, Fancy, Dc3.
Costume, Historical, H8.
Costumes, H8.
Cottages, Fa4.

Cotton, Agriculture, Af6.
Cotton, Dyeing, Um9.
Cotton Manufacture, Um8.
Cough, Me3.
Counterfeits, Law, Jc.
Counterfeits, Money, Se7.
Counter-Irritation, M3.
Counterpoint, Music, Fm1.
Country, Homes, Fa4.
Country, Life, A9.
Courage, Ep5.
Coursing, Fs9.
Court Fools, H8.
Court Houses, Fa3.
Court Law, Jt.
Courtesy, E7.
Courts, Ecclesiastical, Ja.
Courts-martial, Jm.
Courts, Trial, Jt.
Courtship, Ep6.
Covenanters, Tc5.
Cowardice, Ep5.
Cows, A4.
Crabs, Zoology, Nh6.
Crafts, Art, Fd6.
Cramp, Disease, M3.
Cranberries, Ag3.
Cranes, Engineering, Ue3.
Craniology, N2.
Crayfish, Zoology, Nh6.
Crayon Drawing, Fd2.
Creation, Evolution, Mb.
Creation, Metaphysics, Ep2.
Creation, Nature, N.
Creation, Theology, Tc1.
Creator, T5.
Credit, Banking, Se8.
Credit, Companies, Se9.
Credit, National, Se7.
Credo, Fm5.
Cree Indians, Hu1.
Creeds, T8.
Cremation, Mh9.

Crests, Bc2.

Crete, History, Hk5.

Cribbage, Cards, Fs3.

Cricket, Fs1.

Crickets, Nh4.

Crime, Law, Jc.

Crime, Social Science, S3.

Crimea, History, Hrl.

Crimean War, Hr.

Criminal Law, Jt.

Criminals, S3.

Criminology, S3.

Crises, Se8.

Criticism, Art, F.

Criticism, Bible, T3.

Criticism, Drama, Lp2.

Criticism, Literary, Lb3.

Croatia, History, Hg3.

Crocheting, Dc5.

Croquet, Fs8.

Cross, T8.

Croup, Me5.

Crowns, H8.

Crozier, T8.

Crucifix, T8.

Crucifixion, T5.

Cruelty, Ep5.

Crusades, H3.

Crustacea, Nh6.

Cubes, Pm4.

Cyanides, Pc9.

Cyprus, History, Hk5.

Cryptogamia, Nh1.

Cryptography, Eb2.

Crypts, Fd7.

Crystallography, Ng.

Cuba, History, Ha7.

Cuba, Voyages and Travels, Va6.

Culture, Education, E.

Culture, Ethics, E5.

Culture, Law, J.

Culture, Medicine, M.

Culture, Music, Fm2.

Culture, Religion, T1.

Cuneiform Writing, Ek9.

Cupping, M3.

Curacao (Curacoa) History, Ha4.

Cures, M3.

Cures, Miracles, T5.

Curling, Sports, Fs8.

Currency, Se8.

Currents, Atmosphere, Ng7.

Currents, Electric, Pe2.

Curves, Geometry, Pm4.

Customs, Commerce, C4.

Cutaneous Diseases, M4.

Cutlery, Um1.

Cyanides, Pc9.

Cyanides, Poisons, M7.

Cyclades, Hc7.

Cylinders, Drawing, Fd5.

Cycling, Fs8.

Cyclones, Ng7.

Cyclopedias, Gr2.

Cyclops, Nh6.

Cymbals, Fm8.

Cyprus, History, Hc7.

—D—

Daguerreotype, Fp.

Dahlia, Ag5.

Dahomey, History, Ho6.

Dairy, A4.

Dakota, U.S. Hu9.

Dalmatia, History, Hg4.

Damaraland, History, Ho7.

Damascus, History, Hc7.

Dams, Engineering, Ue8.

Dance, Indian, H8.

Dance, Music, Fm4.

Dancing, Fs4.

Dancing, Ethics, Ep5.
Dancing, History, Fs4.
Dangerous Classes, Jt.
Daniel, Bible, T2.
Danish Architecture, Fa1.
Danish Language, Ek5.
Danish Literature, L6.
Danish Mythology, Tn7.
Danish West Indians, History, Ha5.
Danube River, H8.
Danzig, History, Hg1.
Dark Ages, H3.
Dartmore, England, Hb1.
Darwinism, Mb2.
Dates, H6.
Day of Judgment, T6.
Days, Na9.
Dead, Mh9.
Dead Sea, Hc9.
Deaf and Dumb, Education of, E4.
Deafness, Me1.
Death, Future Life, T6.
Death, Hygiene, Mh9.
Death Penalty, Jt.
Death Rate, Mh9.
Debates, Rules, Jr.
Debates, Rhetoric, Ek2.
Debating, Lo.
Debt, Ethics, Ep4.
Debtor, Law, Js.
Debts, Public, Se7.
Decalogue, T2.
Deccan, History, Hc5.
Decimal System, Pm5.
Declamation, Ek2.
Declaration of Independence, U.S. Sp3.
Declaration of War, Jn.
Decoration and Ornament, Fd4.
Decoration, Art, Fd6.
Decoration, House, Fa8.

Decoration, Interior, Fd4.
Decoration, Useful Arts, Ub6.
Decoration Day, H8.
Dedication of Churches, TS.
Deeds, Js.
Deer, Sports, Fs9.
Deer, Zoology, Nh8.
Deformities, Ms.
Degeneration, M6.
Deism, Tc1.
Deism, Deity, T5.
Delaware, U.S. Hu9.
Delaware Indians, History, Hul.
Delhi, History, Hc5.
Deluge, T3.
Delusions, Ep9.
Demand and Supply, Se4.
Democracy, Sp2.
Demonology, Theology, T6.
Demonology, Witchcraft, Ep9.
Denali, Mount McKinley, Ha1.
Denmark, Army and Navy, Hd2.
Denmark, General History, Hd.
Denmark, Separate Places, Hd1.
Denmark, Voyages and Travels, Vd.
Denominations, Tc.
Density, P3.
Density, Astronomy, Na.
Dentistry, Ms7.
Depravity, Philosophy, Ep2.
Depravity, Theology, T6.
Derbyshire, England, Hb1.
Dermatology, M4
Derricks, Ue3.
Dervishes, Tn3.
Descent, Bc.
Descent, Evolution, Mb.
Deserts, Ng8.
Descriptive, Geometry, Pm4.
Design, Ornament, Fd4.
Despotism, Sp1.
Desserts, D3

Detectives, Sg8.

Determinants, Pm3.

Detroit, Michigan, U.S. Hu9.

Deuteronomy, Bible, T2.

Development, Evolution, Mb.

Devices, See Subjects Treated.

Devil, T6.

Devonshire, England, Hb1.

Devotion, T8.

Devotional Exercises, T8.

Devotional, Theology, T9.

Dew, Ng7.

Diabetes, M3.

Diagnosis, M3.

Dialects, Ek4.

Dialogues, Lp4.

Dials, Na9.

Diamonds, Mineralogy, Ng6.

Diamonds, Precious Stones, Fe7.

Diarrhoea, Disease, M3.

Diatomaceae, Nh6.

Dice, Fs3.

Dictionaries, English, Gr3.

Dictionaries, French, Gr5.

Dictionaries, German, Gr4.

Dictionaries, Greek, Gr8.

Dictionaries, Italian, Gr6.

Dictionaries, Latin, Gr7.

Dictionaries, Portuguese, Gr6.

Dictionaries, Spanish, Gr6.

Dictionaries, Others, Gr9.

Die-casting Machines, Ue3.

Die Stamping, Fd8.

Dies, Fe3.

Diet, Mf1.

Differential, Calculus, Pm3.

Digestion, Mf1.

Dikes, Engineering, Ue8.

Dikes, Geology, Ng.

Dining, D2.

Dinners, D2.

Diocesan, History, Tc.

Diphtheria, M3.

Diplomacy, Jn.

Diplomatics, Ek2.

Directories, Gr.

Directory, French, History, Hf.

Disasters, at Sea, V9.

Disasters, Physical Geography, Ng8.

Disciples of Christ, Tc7.

Discourses, See Subjects.

Discoveries, Geographic, V4.

Discoveries, Scientific, U3.

Discoveries, Voyages, V4.

Diseases, Animals, A6.

Diseases, Children, Mg4.

Diseases, Ear, Me1.

Diseases, Eye, Me2.

Diseases, General, M3.

Diseases, Insanity, M6.

Diseases, Lung, Me5.

Diseases, Nervous System, M5.

Diseases, Obstetrics, Mg2.

Diseases, Plants, Nh1.

Diseases, Skin, M4.

Diseases, Stomach, Mf2.

Diseases, Teeth, Ms7.

Diseases, Throat, Me5.

Diseases, Venereal, Mg9.

Diseases, Women, Mg2.

Disfranchisement, Sp.

Disinfection, Mh9.

Dislocation, Ms.

Dispensaries, M1.

Disposal of Dead, Mh9.

Disposal, Sewage, Ub8.

Dissection, Anatomy, Ma1.

Dissection, Ethics, Ep5.

Dissenters, Tc3.

Distillation, Db.

Distillation, Chemistry, Pc9.

Distribution of Animals and Plants, Nh.

District of Columbia, U.S. Hu9.

Divination, Ep9.

Divine, Providence, T5.
Diving Bell, Ue8.
Divinity, T5.
Divinity Schools, T.
Divorce, Ethics, Ep6.
Divorce, Law, Jp.
Divorce, Social Science, S7.
Dixie, U.S. Hu9.
Dixie, Civil War, Hu6.
Docks, Engineering, Ue6.
Doctors, Biography, B.
Doctrinal Theology, T4.
Doctrines, Tc.
Documents, R.
Dog, Domestic Animals, A3.
Dog, Stories, Nh9.
Dog, Zoology, Nh8.
Dogmatic, Theology, T4.
Dolomites, History, Hg4.
Domes, Church, Fa2.
Domes, Domestic Buildings, Fa4.
Domes, Public Buildings, Fa3.
Domestic Animals, A3.
Domestic Architecture, Fa4.
Domestic Economy, D.
Domestic Education, E.
Domestic Law, Jp.
Domestic Medicines, M8.
Domestic Philosophy, Ep6.
Domestic Relations, Jp.
Domestic Science, D.
Domestication, Nh.
Domestics, D.
Dominican Republic, History, Ha6.
Dominicans, Te2.
Dominoes, Fs3.
Doors, Fa.
Doubt, Ep2.
Drafting, See Drawing.
Dragon Flies, Nh4.
Drainage, Agriculture, Af1.
Drainage, Engineering, Ue8.
Drainage, Sanitary, Ub8.

Drama, Lp.
Drama, Amateur, Lp4.
Drama, Collections, Lp3.
Drama, Dramatic Criticism, Lp1.
Drama, English, Lp2.
Drama, French, Lp5.
Drama, General, Lp1.
Drama, German, Lp6.
Drama, Greek, Lp7.
Drama, Italian, Lp9.
Drama, Latin, Lp7.
Drama, Spanish, Lp5.
Drama, Swedish, Lp9.
Draughts, Fs3.
Drawing, Anatomical, Fd5.
Drawing, Architectural, Fd3.
Drawing, Engineering, Fd3.
Drawing, Essays, Fd.
Drawing, Freehand, Fd2.
Drawing, Geometrical, Fd3.
Drawing, Linear, Fd5.
Drawing, Machine, Fd3.
Drawing, Mathematics, Pm9.
Drawing, Mechanical, Fd3.
Drawing, Ornamental, Fd4.
Drawing, Practical, Fd1.
Drawing, Topographical, Fd3.
Dreams, Ep9.
Dredging, Ue8.
Dress, Church, T8.
Dress, Clothing, Dc.
Dress, Ethics, Ep5.
Dress, Manners and Customs, H8.
Dressmaking, Dc1.
Drilling, Engineering, Uc2.
Drill, Mining, Ue9.
Drinking Customs, Ethics, Ep4.
Drinking Customs, Intemperance, M7.
Drinks, Db9.
Driving, Fs8.
Drowning, M8.
Drugs, M1.

Drugs, Ethics, Ep4.
Drunkenness, M7.
Druses, Tn3.
Dry-docks, Ue8.
Dublin, Ireland, Hb2.
Dueling, Ethics, Ep5.
Dueling, Law, Jt.
Dueling, Manners and Customs, H8.
Duets, Vocal, Fm3.
Dumb, Education of, E4.
Dust, Mh1.
Dutch, East Indies, History, Hc3.
Dutch Guiana, History, Ha8.
Dutch, History, Hg9.

Dutch Reformed Church, Tc6.
Duties, Se.
Duties, Servants, D.
Duty, Ep5.
Dwarfs, N2.
Dyaks, History, Hc3.
Dyeing, Um9.
Dyes, Um9.
Dykes, Engineering, Ue8.
Dykes, Geology, Ng.
Dynamics, P3.
Dynamometer, P3.
Dynamos, Pe4.
Dyspepsia, Mf2.

—E—

Eagles, Nh7.
Ear, Me1.
Early Christian Fathers, Br1.
Early Printed Books, G9.
Earth, Ng1
Earth, Astronomy, Na3.
Earth, Physical Geography, Ng8.
Earthenware, Ceramics, Fc.
Earthenware, Manufactures, Um4.
Earthquakes, Ng.
Earths' Surface, Ng1.
Earthwork, Ue9.
Earthworks, Cm1.
Easements. Jp.
East Africa, History, Ho4.
East Indies, History, Hc3.
Easter, Calendar, Na9.
Easter, Ceremonies, T8.
Easter, Music, Fm5.
Easter Island, History, Hc2.
Eastern Churches, Tc2.
Eastern Question, Ho.
Eating, Mf.
Eating Customs, H8.
Ecce Deus, T5.

Ecclesiastes, Bible, T2.
Ecclesiastical Antiquities, Tc.
Ecclesiastical Architecture, Fa2.
Ecclesiastical Art, T8.
Ecclesiastical Biography, Br.
Ecclesiastical Ceremonies, T8.
Ecclesiastical Costume, T8.
Ecclesiastical Fasts and Feasts, T8.
Ecclesiastical Furniture, T8.
Ecclesiastical History, Tc.
Ecclesiastical Law, Ja.
Ecclesiastical Polity, Tc.
Ecclesiastical Vestments, T8.
Ecclesiasticus, Bible, T2.
Eclipses, Na.
Economy, Political, Sp.
Economy, Sociology, Se.
Ecuador, History, Ha8.
Eczema, M4.
Eddas, Lp9.
Eddas, Mythology, Tn7.
Eden, T4.
Edict of Nantes, Tc6.
Edinburgh, Scotland, Hb3.

Editorial, Lb2.

Education, Art, F6.

Education, General Works, E.

Education, History, El.

Education, Industrial, E4.

Education, Physical, Mp.

Education, Self, E5.

Education, Technical, E4.

Education, Vocational, E4.

Efficiency, Eb1.

Eggs, Birds, Nh7.

Egoism, Ethics, Ep5.

Egypt, Art, F9.

Egypt, General History, He.

Egypt, Language, Ek9.

Egypt, Mythology, Tn6.

Egypt, Philosophy, Ep1.

Egypt, Separate Places, Hel.

Egypt, Voyages and Travels, Ve.

Einstein Theory, Pm.

Elasticity, P.

Election, Sp.

Electric Batteries, Pe2.

Electric Bells, Pe7.

Electric Currents, Pe2.

Electric Engineering, Pe3.

Electric Heat, Pe8.

Electric Lamps, Pe6.

Electric Light, Pe6.

Electric Machinery, Pe3.

Electric Measurement, Pe.

Electric Motors, Pe4.

Electric Potential, Pe.

Electric Railroads, Pe5.

Electric Telegraph, Pe8.

Electric Telephone, Pe8.

Electric Testing, Pe.

Electric Transformers, Pe2.

Electric Waves, Pe2.

Electric Welding, Um1.

Electric Wiring, Pe7.

Electricity, Pe.

Electrodynamics, Pe4.

Electrochemistry, Pc.

Electrolysis, Pe2.

Electromagnets, Pe1.

Electrometallurgy, Pe2.

Electroplating, Pe2.

Electrotherapeutics, Pe9.

Electrotyping, Fd8.

Elegiac Poetry, Lp2.

Elephants, Nh8.

Elevator, Engineering, Ue3.

Elevators, Architecture, Fa3.

Elevators, Machinery, Ue3.

Elgin, Scotland, Hb5.

Elizabethan Drama, Lp1.

Ellice Islands, History, Hel.

Ellipse, Pm4

Elocution, Lo.

Eloquence, Lo.

Elves, H8.

Emancipation, S6.

Embalming, Mh9.

Embankments, Ue6.

Embargo Laws, Jm.

Emblems, T8.

Embossing, Book, Ut7.

Embroidery, Dc5.

Embryology, Botany, Nh1.

Embryology, Zoology, Nh3.

Emetics, M8.

Emergencies, M8.

Emigration, Se3.

Emotions, Ep4.

Emulation, Se3.

Enamel, Fd6.

Encylopaedias, Gr2.

Endless Punishment, T6.

Energy, P6.

Engineering, Civil, Ue6.

Engineering, General Works, Ue.

Engineering, Hydraulic, Ue8.

Engineering, Locomotive, Ue5.

Engineering, Marine, Ue4.

Engineering, Mathematics, Pm9.

Engineering, Mechanical, Ue1.
Engineering, Railroad, Ue7.
Engineering, Steam, Ue5.
Engineering, Topographical, Pm6.
Engineers, Lives, B.
Engines, Gas, Ue3.
Engines, Marine, Ue4.
Engines, Oil, Ue3.
Engines, Turbine, Ue3.
England, History, Hb.
England, Church of, Tc3.
English Language, Ek4.
English Literature, L4.
Engravers' Lives, F2.
Engravers' Lives, Collective, F3.
Engravings, Fe1.
Engravings, Catalogues, F8.
Enigmas, Fs4.
Ensilage, A4.
Entail, Law, Js.
Enteric Fever, M3.
Entertainments, Private, Fs4.
Entertainments, Public, Lp4.
Entomology, Nh4.
Entozoa, M3.
Environment, Ethics, Ep2.
Environment, Evolution, Mb.
Envy, Ep4.
Ephemerides, Na8.
Ephesians, Bible, T2.
Epic, Poetry, English, Ep2.
Epic, Poetry, Greek, Lp7
Epic, Poetry, Latin, Lp7.
Epicurean Philosophy, Ep1.
Epidemics, Mh9.
Epigrams, Lq.
Epigraphy, Writing, Ek2.
Epilepsy, M5.
Episcopacy, Tc.
Episcopal Church, Tc3.
Epistles, Bible, T2.
Epitaphs, Lb8.
Equations, Algebra, Pm3.

Equations, Chemical, Pc9.
Equations, Trigonometry, Pm6.
Equilibrum, P3.
Equinoxes, Na3.
Equity, Jt.
Erie, New York, U.S. Hu9.
Eritrea, Africa, Ho4.
Erosion, Ng2.
Erratics, Ng.
Errors, Ek3.
Eruptions, Disease, M4.
Eruptions, Volcanic, Ng8.
Erysipelas, Disease, M4.
Escapes, V9.
Eschatology, T6.
Esdras, Bible, T2.
Eskimo, Hn1.
Esoteric Buddhism, Tn1.
Essays, English and American, Le1.
Essays, French, Le4.
Essays, General, Le.
Essays, German, Le6.
Essays, Greek, Le7.
Essays, Indian, Le8.
Essays, Latin, Le7.
Essays, Persian, Le8.
Essays, Portuguese, Le5.
Essays, Spanish, Le5.
Essenes, Tn2.
Essex, England, Hb1.
Essex, Massachusetts, U.S. Hu9.
Esther, Bible, T2.
Esthetics, F1.
Esthetics, Architecture, Fa.
Esthonia, History, Hr.
Estimates, Building, Ub.
Etching, Fe.
Etchings, Catalogues, F8.
Etchings, Pictures, F4.
Eternal Life, T6.
Eternity, T6.
Ether, Pc9.

Ethical Culture, Ep5.
Ethics, Ep5.
Ethiopian Language, Ek9.
Ethnography, N.
Ethnology, N.
Etiquette, E7.
Etruria, History, Hi1.
Etruscan, Architecture, Fa1.
Etudes, Fm1.
Etymology, Ek4.
Eucharist, T8.
Euchre, Fs3.
Eudiometer, Pc.
Eulogies, B.
Euphemism, Ek1.
Europe, History, H3.
Evangelists, Tc9.
Evaporation, Brewing, Db.
Evaporation, Physics, P3.
Evergreens, Botany, Nh1.
Evergreens, Landscape Gardening, Ag7.
Evidence, Law, Jt.
Evidence, Logic, Ep5.
Evidences of Christianity, Tc.
Evidences of the Bible, T2.
Evil, Ethics, Ep4.
Evil, Sin, T6.
Evil Spirits, Theology, T6.
Evil Spirits, Witchcraft, Ep9.
Evolution, Arithmetic, Pm3.
Evolution, Biology, Mb.
Evolution, Philosophy, Ep2.
Evolution, Theology, Tc1.
Examinations, E3.
Excavation, Mining, Ue9.
Excavation, Archaeology, N.

Exchange, Pm8.
Exchange, Banking, Se8.
Excommunication, Tc2.
Executors, Jp.
Exercise, Physical, Mp.
Exhibitions, Art, F8.
Exhibitions, Agricultural, A1.
Exhibitions, General, U.
Exhibitions, School, E.
Ex Libris, Lb1.
Exodus, Bible, T2.
Exorcism, Ep9.
Exotics, Nh1.
Experiments, Chemical, Pc4.
Explorations, V4.
Explorers, Biography, Collective, Bc.
Explorers, Biography, Individual, B.
Explosions, Ue5.
Explosives, Chemistry, Pc9.
Explosives, Mining, Ue9.
Exportations, C4.
Expositions, Agricultural, A1.
Expositions, Fine Arts, F8.
Expositions, Useful Arts, U.
Express Companies, Commerce, C2.
Expression, Art Anatomy, Fd5.
Expression, Musical, Fm1.
Expression, Physiognomy, Ep8.
Extracts, Lq.
Extradition, Jn.
Eye, Disease, Mc2.
Eye, Surgery, Ms.
Ezekiel, Bible, T2.
Ezra, Bible, T2.

—F—

Fables, Lb8.
Fabrics, Um8.
Face, Anatomy, Ma1.

Face, Physiognomy, Ep8.
Face, Surgery, Ms.
Facetiae, Lw.

Factories, Um.

Factory, Labor, Se.

Factory, Management, Eb1.

Faience, Fc.

Fairies, II8.

Fairs, Agricultural, A1.

Fairs, Useful Arts, U.

Fairy Tales, English Literature, L1.

Fairy Tales, Manners and Customs, H8.

Faith, Philosophy, Ep2.

Faith, Theology, T6.

Faith Cure, Ep9.

Falconry, Fs9.

Falkland Islands, History, Ha6.

Fall, Nh.

Fall of Man, T6.

Fallacies, Ep3.

Falling Stars, Na2.

Fallopian Tube, Disease, Mg2.

Falls, Ng9.

Falsehood, Ep5.

Fame, Ep4.

Families, Bc3.

Family, Ethics, Ep6.

Family, Law, Jp.

Family, Philosophy, Ep6.

Family, Prayer, T8.

Famines, Disease, M3.

Famines, Hygiene, Mh1.

Fan, Dc.

Fanaticism, Ep9.

Fancy Costumes, Dc3.

Fancy Drawing, Fd2.

Fancy Work, Dc5.

Farces, Lp2.

Farm Houses, Architecture, Fa4.

Farming, Af.

Faroe Islands, History, Ha1.

Farriery, Shoeing, Ut4.

Farriery, Veterinary Science, A6.

Fashion, Costume, Dc3.

Fashion, Manners, and Customs, H8.

Fasting, Mf9.

Fasts and Feasts, T8.

Fate, Ep9.

Fathers, Ethics, Ep6.

Fathers of the Church, Biography, Br.

Fatigue, Mh5.

Fats, Chemistry, Pc9.

Fats, Oils, Um6.

Fauces, Disease, M5.

Fauna, Nh3.

Fayence, Fc.

Fear, Disease, M5.

Fear, Philosophy, Ep3.

Feasts, Church, T8.

Feasts, Manners and Customs, H8.

Fecundation, Botany, Nh2.

Fecundation, Zoology, Nh3.

Fecundity, Mg3.

Federal Government, Sp.

Feeble-minded, Insanity, M6.

Feeble-minded, Hospitals, M8.

Feelings, Ep4.

Feet, Anatomy, Ma1.

Feet, Hygiene, Mh8.

Feet, Surgery, Ms.

Felony, Jt.

Felt Manufacture, Um8.

Female, Advice to, Mg3.

Fences, Law, Jp.

Fencing, Fs1.

Fenians, Secret Societies, H9.

Fermentation, Chemistry, Pc.

Fermentation, Foods, M2.

Ferns, Ag8.

Ferns, Botany, Nh2.

Ferries, C2.

Fertilization, Botany, Nh1.

Fertilizers, Af1.

Festivals, Church, T8.

Festivals, Manners and Customs, H8.

Fetishism, Tn4.

Feudal-Law, Ja.

Feudalism, Sp.

Fever, M3.

Fibres, Agriculture, Af2.

Fibres, Manufacture, Um8.

Fiction, L1.

Fictitious Names, G2.

Fiddle, Fm8.

Fidelity, Ep4.

Field Sports, Fs1.

Fighting, Fs1.

Figure of the Earth, Astronomy, Na3.

Figure of the Earth, Geodesy, Na7.

Figure Painting, Fd5.

Fiji Islands, History, Hc2.

Filibusters, Law, Jt.

Filices, Nh2.

Filing, Machines, Eb9.

Filing, Systems, Eb.

Filth, Hygiene, Mh.

Filtration, Sewage, Ue8.

Filtration, Water, Mh1.

Finance, Se8.

Finding Lists, G5.

Fine Arts, F.

Finger Prints, S3.

Finger Rings, Jewelry, Fe8.

Finger Rings, Manners and Customs, H8.

Finite, Ep2.

Finland, History, Hr2.

Finland, Language, Ek9.

Finland, Literature, L9.

Fire, Uf2.

Fire Departments, Sg9.

Fire Engine, Ue3.

Fire Insurance, C7.

Fireplaces, Ub9.

Fire Worshipers, Tn4.

Firearms, Army, Cm1.

Firearms, Manufacture, Ut2.

Firearms, Navy, Cn1.

Fires, Uf2.

Fireworks, Pc9.

Fish, Nh6.

Fish Culture, Nh6.

Fisheries, Nh6.

Fishing, Fs7.

Fiume, History, Hg3.

Flagellants, Tc2.

Flageolet, Fm8.

Flags, Heraldry, Bc9.

Flags, Manufacture, Um8.

Flames, P3.

Flanders, History, Hg8.

Flattery, Ep4.

Flax, Af6.

Flemish, Art, F5.

Flemish, Architecture, Fa1.

Flemish, Language, Ek9.

Flemish, Literature, L9.

Flies, Nh4.

Flogging, Jt.

Floods, Ng7.

Floors, Architecture, Fa.

Flora, Nh1.

Florence, History, Hi1.

Florence, Voyages and Travels, Vi.

Florescence, P2.

Floriculture, Ag5.

Florida, U.S. Hu9.

Flour Manufacture, Um5.

Flower Painting, Fd1.

Flowers, Botany, Nh1.

Flowers, Gardening, Ag5.

Fluids, P8.

Flute, Fm8.

Fluxions, Pm3.

Flying, P9.

Flying Machines, P9.

Fog, Ng7.

Foliage, Nh1.

Folk Lore, Manners and Customs, H8.

Folk Lore, Mythology, Tn7-8-9.

Folk Songs, Music, Fm3.

Fonts, T8.

Food, Mf.

Food, Adulteration, Mf1.

Food, Chemistry, Pc7.

Food, Cookery, D3.

Food, Digestion, Mf1.

Fools, Ep4.

Foot, Mh8.

Football, Fs1.

Footprints, Fossils, Ng4.

Force, Ethics, Ep2.

Force, Mechanics, P3.

Foreclosure, Law, Jp.

Foreign Exchange, Pm8.

Foreign Missions, Tc9.

Foremanship, Eb1.

Forensic Law, Jp.

Foreordination, T6.

Forest Trees, Nh2.

Forestry, Af9.

Forge, Um1.

Forgery, Law, Jp.

Formosa, History, Hc.

Forms, Social, E7.

Fortification, Cm1.

Fortune Telling, Ep9.

Fossil, Footprints, Ng4.

Fossils, Ng3.

Fossils, Animal, Ng5.

Fossils, Man, Ng4.

Fossils, Plant, Ng5.

Foundations, Building, Ub1.

Foundations, Cement, Ub2.

Founding, Ue2.

Fountains, Ag6.

Fowl, A7.

Fowling, Fs9.

Fox, Nh8.

Fractions, Pm3.

Fracture, Ms.

Framing, Carpentry, Ub4.

France, History, Hf.

France, Army and Navy, Hf4.

France, Separate Places, Hf1.

France, Voyages and Travels, V

Franciscans, Tc1.

Franconia, History, Hg5.

Frankfort, History, Hg1.

Fraud, Jp.

Free Agency, T6.

Free Churches, Tc.

Free Institutions, S9.

Free Religion, Tc1.

Free Schools, E1.

Free Speech, Se.

Free Thought, Tc1.

Free Trade, Se.

Free Will, Sp2.

Freebooters, Jt.

Freedman, S6.

Freedom, Slavery, S6.

Freedom of the Press, Se.

Freedom of the Will, Ep2.

Freehand Drawing, Fd2.

Freemasonry, H9.

Freezing, Machines, Ue3.

Freezing, Physics, P3.

Freight, Commerce, C2.

French Africa, History, Ho3.

French Guinea, Africa, Ho7.

French India, Asia, Hc4.

French Language, Ek6.

French Literature, L5.

French Revolution, Hf.

Fresco Painting, Fd4.

Fret Cutting, Fa6.

Friars, Tc2.

Friction, Ue1.

Friendly Islands, History, Hc2.

Friendly Societies, S9.

Friends, Society of, Tc8.

Friendship, Ep4.

Froebel's Educational System, E3.
Frogs, Nh6.
Frost, Ng8.
Fruit, Agriculture, Ag3.
Fruit, Preserves, D3.
Fuchow, History, Hc.
Fuel, Uf.
Fague, Music, Fm1.
Fumigation, Mh9.

Funds, Se8.
Funerals, H8.
Fungi, Nh1.
Furniture, Architecture, Fa6.
Furniture, Domestic Economy, D9.
Furniture, Manufacture, Um.
Furs, Dc2.
Future Life, T6,
Future Punishment, T6.

—G—

Gaelic Language, Ek9.
Gaelic Literature, L9.
Gaging, Pm5.
Galatians, Bible, T2.
Galatia, History, Hc7.
Gales, Ng7.
Galicia, Austria, Hg3.
Galicia, Spain, Hs1.
Gall, Disease, M3.
Gallantry, E7.
Gallas, History, Ho4.
Galleys, Ja.
Gallows, Law, Jt.
Galvanism, Pe2.
Galvanizing, Manufacture, Um1.
Galvanometer, Pe.
Galvanoplasty, Pe2.
Gambia, Africa, Ho6.
Gambling, Ethics, Ep4.
Gambling, Law, J.
Game, Laws, Fs9.
Game, Sports, Fs9.
Games, Indoor, Fs4.
Games, Outdoor, Fs1.
Gaming, Ep4.
Garbage, Mh1.
Gardening, Ag.
Gardens, Landscape, Ag6.
Gardens, Ornamental, Ag6.
Gas, Uf.

Gas, Analysis, Pc3.
Gas, Engine, Ue3
Gas, Fitting, Ub8.
Gas, Heating, Ub9.
Gas, Lighting, Uf1.
Gas, Physics, P5.
Gas, Sewer, Mh1.
Gases, Uf1.
Gasoline, Um6.
Gastritis, Disease, Mf1.
Gastronomy, D3.
Gauging, Pm5.
Gaul, History, Hf.
Gazetteers, V1.
Gearing, Ue1.
Gelatine, Process, Photography,
   Fp4.
Gems, Geology, Ng.
Gems, Jewelry, Fe7.
Gems, Mineralogy, Ng6.
Genealogy, Bc2-7.
Generation, Botany, Nh1.
Generation, Female, Mg3.
Generation, Male, Mg8.
Genesis, Bible, T2.
Geneva, History, Hf9.
Genii, H8.
Genius, Ep2.
Genoa, History, Hi1.
Gentleness, Ethics, Ep6.

Gentleness, Etiquette, E7.

Geochemistry, Ng.

Geodesy, Na7.

Geodetic, Surveying, Pm6.

Geographical Distibution, Animal, Nh3.

Geographical Distribution, Plants, Nh1.

Geographical Names, Bc8.

Geographical Societies, S9.

Geography, V1.

Geography, Ancient, H2.

Geography, Descriptive, V1.

Geography, Historical, H8.

Geography, Physical, Ng8.

Geological Reports, Ng.

Geological Surveys, Ng.

Geology, Ng.

Geology, Glacial Period, Ng2.

Geometrical Drawing, Fd3.

Geometry, Pm4.

Georgia, U.S. Hu9.

Germ Theory, M2.

German East Africa, History, Ho4.

German Language, Ek5.

German Literature, L6.

German Mythology, Tn7.

Germany, Army and Navy, Hg2.

Germany, General History, Hg.

Germany, Seperate Places, Hg1.

Germany, Voyages and Travels, Vg.

Germination, Nh1.

Gesture, Lo.

Gettysburg, Pa. U.S. Hu9.

Geysers, Ng1.

Ghent, History, Hg8.

Ghost, Holy, T5.

Ghosts, Ep9.

Giants, N2.

Gibralter, History, Hs1.

Gilbert Islands, History, Hc2.

Gilding, Brass, Etc. Um2.

Gilds, Se1.

Gilead, Voyages and Travels, Vc7.

Gipsies, H8.

Girders, Engineering, Ue6.

Girls, Advice to, Mg3.

Girls, Ethics, Ep5.

Girondists, History, Hf.

Glaciers, Ng2.

Gladiators, H8.

Glanders, A6.

Glasgow, Scotland, Hb5.

Glass Manufacture, Um4.

Glass Painting, Fc.

Glass Stained, Fc2.

Glazing, Uc7.

Glees, Music, Fm3.

Globes, Na.

Gloves, Clothing, Dc.

Gloves, Manufacture, Ut8.

Glucose, Um5.

Glue Manufacture, Um5.

Glycerine, Pc9.

Glyphography, Fc3.

Goat, A4.

Goblins, H8.

God, T5.

Gods, Tn5.

Golden Fleece, Tn8.

Gold Coast, History, Ho6.

Gold, Coinage, Se7.

Gold, Finance, Se7.

Gold, Jewelry, Fe8.

Gold, Metallurgy, Ue9.

Gold, Mineralogy, Ng6.

Gold, Money, Fe5.

Glodsmithing, Fe8.

Golf, Fs8.

Gonorhoea, Mg9.

Good Friday, T8.

Good Hope, Cape of, Ho7.

Goodness, Ep6.

Gorilla, Nh8.

Gospels, T2.

Gossip, Ep4.
Gothic Architecture, Fa1.
Goths, History, Hg.
Gout, M3.
Government, Sg.
Governors' Lives, B.
Grace, Art, F1.
Grace, Saving, T6.
Grafting, Ag.
Grain, Af2.
Graining, Ub6.
Grammer, English, Ek4.
Grammer, French, Ek6.
Grammer, German, Ek5.
Grammer, Greek, Ek8.
Grammer, Italian, Ek7.
Grammer, Latin, Ek8.
Grammer, Norwegian, Ek5.
Grammer, Portuguese, Ek7.
Grammer, Swedish, Ek5.
Grammer Schools, E1.
Granada, History, Hs1.
Grand Islands, Vermont, U.S. Hu9.
Grand Rapids, Michigan, U.S. Hu9.
Grangers, Sp.
Granite, Ub1.
Grape Culture, Ag3.
Graphic Arts, Fd8.
Graphics, Drawing, Fd3.
Graphite, Ng.
Graphology, Ep7.
Grass, Nh2.
Grasshoppers, Nh4.
Gratitude, Ep6.
Gravel, Building, Ub2.
Gravel, Disease, M3.
Gravestones, Fd7.
Graveyards, Ag7.
Gravitation, Astronomy, Na.
Gravitation, Mechanics, P3.
Gravitation, System, Ue8.
Grazing, A4.

Great Britain, Army and Navy, Hb7.
Great Britain, Government, Sp4.
Great Britain, History, Hb.
Great Britain, Separate Places, Hb1.
Great Britain, Voyages and Travels, Vb.
Great Salt Lake, Utah, U.S. Hu9.
Great War, 1914-1920, Sp.
Greece, History, Hk5.
Greece, Voyages and Travels, Vk5.
Greek, Architecture, Fa1.
Greek Art, F9.
Greek Church, Tc2.
Greek Language, Ek8.
Greek Literature, L7.
Greek Philosophy, Ep1.
Greek Sculpture, Fd7.
Greenbacks, Se7.
Greenhouses, Ag.
Greenland, History, Ha1.
Greenland, Voyages and Travels, Va1.
Grinding Machines, Ue3.
Grippe, La, M3.
Grotesque, F1.
Grottoes, Ng8.
Groves, Ag6.
Guadeloupe, History, Ha6.
Guam, Pacific, Hc2.
Guano. Af1.
Guaranties and Sureties, Js.
Guardians, Js.
Guatemala, History, Ha4.
Guernsey Islands, History, Hc1.
Guiana, History, Ha8.
Guide Books, General, V2.
Guide Books, See Under Countries.
Guienne, History, Hf1.
Guilds, Se1.
Guillotine, Jt.
Guinea, History, Ho6.

Guitar, Fm8.

Gums, Manufacture, Um5.

Gun Making, Ut2.

Guncotton, Pc9.

Gunnery, Cm1.

Gunning, Fs9.

Gunpowder, Pc9.

Gutta Percha, Um5.

Gymnastics, Mp.

Gynecology, Mg1.

Gypsies, H8.

Gypsum, Af1.

—H—

Habakkuk, Bible, T2.

Habeas Corpus, Jp.

Habit, Ep2.

Habitations, Animal, Nh3.

Habitation, Hygiene, Mh.

Habits, H8.

Hackensack, New Jersey, U.S. Hu9.

Hades, T6.

Haggai, Bible, T2.

Hague, History, Hg9.

Hague Treaty, Sp.

Hail, Ng7.

Hair Goods, Um3.

Hair, Hygiene, Mh6.

Hair, Toilet, Dc8.

Halifax, Nova Scotia, History, Ha2.

Hall Marks, Fe9.

Hallucinations, Ep9.

Hamburg, History, Hg1.

Hand, Anatomy, Ma1.

Hand, Hygiene, Mh7.

Hand, Palmistry, Ep7.

Handicraft, Ut.

Handrailing, Ub4.

Handwriting, Ep7.

Hanging, Jt.

Happiness, Ep6.

Harbors, Engineering, Ue8.

Hardware, Um1.

Harmonics, Pm4.

Harmony, Fm1.

Harness, Ut6.

Harps, Fm8.

Hartford, Conn., U.S. Hu9.

Hatching, A7.

Hate, Ep4.

Hats, Ut8.

Havana, Cuba, History, Ha7.

Hawaii, History, Hc2.

Hawking, Fs9.

Hay Fever, M3.

Hayti, History, Ha6.

Haze, Ng7.

Head, Mh6.

Head, Surgery, Ms.

Headache, M5.

Head gear, H8.

Headstones, Fd7.

Healing, Ep9.

Health, Mh.

Health Resorts, M9.

Hearing, Accoustics, P4.

Hearing, Disease, Me1.

Heart, M3.

Hearts, Cards, Fs3.

Heat, Engines, Ue3.

Heat, Physics, P3.

Heathen, Missions, Tc9.

Heating, Ub9.

Heatstroke, M3.

Heaven, T6.

Heavens, Astronomy, Na.

Hebrew, History, Hc8.

Hebrew, Language, Ek9.

Hebrew, Literature, L9.

Hebrew, Religion, Tn2.

Hebrews, Epistles to the Bible, T2.

Hebribes, History, Hb4.

Hedges, Ag7.

Heidelberg, History, Hg1.

Heliometer, Na.

Heliotypes, Fp8.

Hell, T6.

Helmets, Cm1.

Hemorrhage, M3.

Hemorrhoids, M3.

Hemp, Agriculture, Af6.

Hemp, Manufacture, Um8.

Hens, A7.

Heraldry, Bc2-7.

Herculaneum, History, Hi.

Heredity, Mb3.

Heresy, Tc1.

Hermaphrodites, Animal, Nh3.

Hermaphrodites, Human, N2.

Hermeneutics, T2.

Hermetic Art, Pc1.

Hernia, Disease, M3.

Hernia, Surgery, Ms.

Heroism, Ep5.

Herpetology, Nh6.

Herzegovina, History, Hg4.

Hesse-Darmstadt, History, Hg1.

Hessians, History, U. S. Revolution, Hu4.

Hexagons, Pm4.

Hidalgo, History, Ha5.

Hieroglyphics, Ek1.

High Schools, E1.

Highwaymen, Jt.

Highways, Engineering, Ue6.

Highways, Law, Js.

Highways, Transportation, C2.

Himalaya Mountains, Vc5.

Hindu Language, Ek9.

Hindu Philosophy, Ep1.

Hindu Religion, Tn1.

Hindustan, History, Hc5.

Hippodrome, Fs2.

Histology, Ma.

Historians, Lives, B.

Historical Atlases, H5.

Historical Costumes, H8.

Historical Dictionaries, H5.

Historical Societies, H1.

History, H.

History, Ancient, H2.

History, Christianity, Tc.

History, Essays, H.

History, Medieaval, H3.

History, Modern, H3.

History, Natural, Nh.

History, Philosophy of, H7.

History, Universal, H4.

Historionics, Lp1.

Hittites, History, Hc7.

Hivaoa Islands, History, Hc3.

Hives, Disease, M4.

Hoarseness, Me4.

Hoboken, N.J. U.S. Hu9.

Hockey, Fs8.

Hog, A4.

Hoisting Engines, Ue3.

Holidays, Manners and Customs, H8.

Holidays, School, E.

Holiness, T4.

Holland, History, Hg4.

Holland, Voyages and Travels, Vg9.

Hollow Tile Construction, Ub1.

Hollow Tile Manufacture, Um4.

Holy Bible, T2.

Holy Ghost, T5.

HolyLand, History, Hc7.

Holy Land, Voyages and Travels, Vc7.

Holy Roman Empire, Hg.

Holy Spirit, T5.

Holy Week, T8.

Home, Ep6.
Home Decoration, Fa8.
Home Education, E5.
Home Ethics, Ep6.
Home Missions, Tc9.
Homeopathy, M3.
Homes, Architecture, Fa4.
Homes, Sanitation, Uc9.
Homicide, Jt.
Homiletics, T7.
Honduras, History, Ha4.
Honesty, Ethics, Ep5.
Honey, A8.
Hong Kong, History, Hc.
Honolulu, History, Hc2.
Honor, Ep5.
Hop Culture, Af2.
Hopkinsianism, Tc6.
Horology, Na9.
Horoscope, Ep9.
Horse, Domestic, A6.
Horse, Zoology, Nh8.
Horse racing, Fs8.
Horse railroads, Ue7.
Horsemanship, Fs8.
Horseshoeing, Ut4.
Horticulture, Ag5.
Hosea, Bible, T2.
Hosiery, Manufacture, Um8.
Hosiery, Toilet, Dc.
Hospitallers, H9.
Hospitals, M8.
Host, T8.
Hotels, D.
Hothouses, Ag.
Hottentots, History, Ho2.
Hour Glass, Na9.
Hours of Labor, Se4.
House Decoration, Fa8.
House Drainage, Ub8.
House Paintings, Ub6.
Household Decorations, Fa8.
Houses, Architecture, Fa.

Housewifery, D.
Hudson's Bay, History, Ha2.
Huguenots, Tc6.
Human Anatomy for Artists, Fd5.
Human Body, Ma1.
Human Faculties, Ep2.
Human Figure, Fd5.
Human Race, N.
Humanity, Ep6.
Humbugs, Ep9.
Humility, Ep6.
Humidity, Ng7.
Humming Birds, Nh7.
Humor, Lw.
Hun, History, Hc9.
Hungary, History, Hg3.
Hunting, Fs9.
Hurricanes, Ng7.
Husband and Wife, Law, Jp.
Husbandry, A.
Husbands, Ep6.
Hussites, Tc6.
Hybrids, Animal, Nh3.
Hybrids, Plants, Nh1.
Hydraulic Engineering, Ue8.
Hydraulic, Machinery, Ue3.
Hydraulics, P8.
Hydrodynamics, Engineering, Ue8.
Hydro-dynamics, Physics, P8.
Hydrogen, Pc5.
Hydrogeology, Ng7.
Hydrography, Pm6.
Hydrology, Ng9.
Hydromechanics, P8.
Hydropathy, M9.
Hydrophobia, M3.
Hydrostatics, P8.
Hydrozoa, Nh6.
Hygiene, Public, Mh1.
Hymnology, T8.
Hymns, Music, Fm5

Hyperbola, Pm4.

Hypnotism, Ep9.

Hypothesis, Ep3.

Hysteria, M5.

—I—

Ice Age, Ng2.

Icebergs, Ng2.

Ice, Hygiene, Mh1.

Ice, Manufacture, Pc9.

Ice, Physical Geography, Ng2.

Iceland, History, Ha1.

Iceland, Voyages and Travels, Va1.

Ichnology, Ng3.

Ichthyology, Nh6.

Iconography, Sacred, T9.

Idaho, U. S. Hu9.

Idealism, Ep2.

Idiocy, Ep4.

Idiosyncracies, Ep4.

Idleness, Ep6.

Idol Bel and the Dragon, Bible, T2.

Idolatry, Mythology, Tn7.

Idolatry, Theology, Tn.

Illinois, U. S., Hu9.

Illiteracy, S4.

Illumination, Decoration, Fd4.

Illumination, Electric, Pe6.

Illusions, Ep9.

Illustration of Books, Fd2.

Image Worship, Mythology, Tn7.

Image, Worship, Theology, Tn.

Imagination, Body, Ep9.

Imagination, Mind, Ep3.

Imbecility, Ep4.

Immaculate Conception, T5.

Immersion, T8.

Immigration, Se3.

Immorality, Ethics, Ep2.

Immorality, Law, Jc.

Immorality, Social Science, S3.

Immorality, Theology, T6.

Imprecations, Ep5.

Imperial Federation, Sp1.

Imports, C.

Imposters, Ep9.

Imprisonment, Jp.

Incandescent Lamps, Pe6.

Incantations, Ep9.

Incarnation, T5.

Incas, History, Ha8.

Incense, T8.

Incest, Law, Jt.

Income Public, Se7.

Income Tax, Economy, Se2.

Income Tax, Locals, Sg1.

Incubation, A7.

Incubus, Ep9.

Incunabula, G9.

Indemnity, Law, Jn.

Independent Order of Odd Fellows, H9.

Independents, Tc6.

Index, G3.

Index, Business, Eb.

India, History, He5.

India, Voyages and Travels, Vc5.

India Rubber, Um5.

Indian Archipelago, Hc3.

Indian Corn, Af6.

Indian Language, Ek9.

Indian Music, Fm3.

Indiana, U. S., Hu9.

Indianapolis, Indiana, U. S. Hu9.

Indians, Mexican, Ha5.

Indians, North American, Hu1.

Indicators, Steam, Ue5.

Indigestion, Mf1.

Indigo, Chemistry, Pc9.

Indigo, Dyeing, Um9.

Indoor Amusements, Fs3.

Invalids, M3.

Inventions, U3.

Invertebrates, Nh3.

Investments, Se8.

Iodine, Pc5.

Ionian Islands, History, Hk5.

Iowa, U. S., Hu9.

Iranic Language, Ek9.

Ireland, History, Hb2-3.

Ireland, Voyages and Travels, Vb2.

Irish Language, Ek9.

Irish Literature, L9.

Iron, Buildings, Ub.

Iron, Bridges, Ue6.

Iron, Manufactures, Um1.

Iron, Metallurgy, Ue9.

Iron, Mineralogy, Ng6.

Iron, Mining, Ue9.

Iron, Ships, Cs.

Iron-Clad Vessels, Naval, Cn9.

Iron-Clad Vessels, Shipbuilding, Cs.

Ironwork, Um1.

Iroquois Indians, History, Ha2.

Irrigation, Engineering, Ue8.

Irrigation, Farming, Af1.

Isaiah, Bible, T2.

Islam, Tn3.

Isle de France, History, Hf1.

Isle of Man, History, Hb4.

Isle of Man, Voyages and Travels, Vb3.

Isle of Wight, History, Hb1.

Israelites, Hc8.

Italian East Africa, Ho4.

Italian Language, Ek7.

Italian Literature, L4.

Italy, History, Hi.

Italy, Army and Navy, Hi7.

Italy, Separate Places, Hi1.

Italy, Voyages and Travels, Vi.

Ivory, Carving, Fd7.

Ivory, Manufacture, Um4.

Ivy, Ag6.

—J—

Jacksonville, Florida, U. S. Hu9.

Jacobins, History, Hf.

Jade, Jewelry, Fg8.

Jade, Mineralogy, Ng6.

Jails, S3.

Jamaica, History, Ha6.

James, Bible, T2.

Jansenists, Tn5.

Japan, History; Hc1.

Japan, Voyages and Travels, Vc1.

Japanese Language, Ek9.

Japanese Literature, L9.

Japanning, Ub6.

Jaundice, Disease, M3.

Java, History, Hc3.

Jealousy, Ep4.

Jeddo, History, Hc1.

Jehovah, T5.

Jelly Fish, Nh6.

Jeremiah, Bible, T2.

Jersey City, New Jersey, U. S. Hu9.

Jerusalem, Hc7.

Jesters, H8.

Jests, Lw.

Jesuits, Tc2.

Jesus, Society of, Tc2.

Jesus Christ, T5.

Jewelry, Manufacture, Fe8.

Jewelry, Ornament, Dc8.

Jewish History, Hc8.

Jewish Language, Ek9.

Jewish Literature, L9.

Jewish Philosophy, Ep1.

Jewish Religion, Tn2.

Job, Book of Bible, T2.

John, Bible, T2.

John, St., Bible, T2.

Joinery, Ub4.

Joints, Diseases of, M3.

Joint Stock Companies, Se1.

Jokes, Lw.

Jonah, Bible, T2.

Joshua, Bible, T2.

Journalism, Lb2.

Journeys, Land, V8.

Journeys, Sea, V3.

Judaism, Tn2.

Jude, Bible, T2.

Judea, History, Hc7.

Judges, Bible, T2.

Judgment, Day of, T6.

Judith, Bible, T2.

Juggernaut, Tn.

Juggling, Fs5.

Jugoslavia, History, Hg4.

Jugurthine War, Hk.

Jupiter, Na2.

Jurisdiction, Jt.

Jurisprudence, J.

Jurisprudence, Medical, Js.

Jury, Jt.

Justice, Ep6.

Justification, Tc.

Jute, Af2.

Juvenile Poetry, Lp4.

—K—

Kabala, Ep1.

Kaffraria, History, Ho7.

Kafirs, History, Ho7.

Kaleidoscope, P2.

Kamerun, History, Ho6.

Kamchatka, History, Hr2.

Kangaroo, Nh3.

Kansas, U. S. Hu9.

Kant, Ep2.

Karlsbad, History, Hg4.

Kartum, He.

Kashmir, Hc5.

Keltic History, Hb2.

Keltic Language, Ek9.

Kentucky, U. S. Hu9.

Keramics, Fc.

Kerosene, Pc9.

Keys, Ut2.

Khartum, He.

Khiva, History, Hc5.

Khiva, Voyages and Travels, Vc5.

Kidnaping, Jt.

Kidneys, M3.

Kindergarten, E3.

Kindness, E7.

Kinematics, P3.

Kinetics, P3.

Kings, Bible, T2.

Kings, Lives, B.

Kinship, Bc.

Kissing, Customs, Ep5.

Kissing, Literature of, L2.

Kitchen, D.

Kitchen Gardening, Ag1.

Kleptomania, M5.

Knight-errantry, H3.

Knighthood, Bc-3-7.

Knights Hospitallers, H9.

Knights of Columbus, H9.

Knights of the Maccabees, H9.

Knights of Malta, H9.

Knights of St. John, H9.

Knights of Trinity, H9.

Knights Templar, H9.

Knitting, Dc.

Knives, Um1.

Knots, Cs.
Know-nothings, Sp3.
Knowledge, Ep3.
Koran, Tn3.

Korea, History, Hc.
Ku-Klux-Klan, History, H9.
Kurdistan History, Hc7.

—L—

Labor, Se4.
Labor, Law, Js.
Laboratory, Chemistry, Pc4.
Labrador, Ha1.
Labyrinths, N.
Lace, Dc5.
Lachrymal Diseases, M3.
Laconia, History, Hk5.
Lacquer, Chemistry, Pc9.
Lacquer Work, Fa6.
Lacrosse, Fs8.
Ladrone Islands, History, Hc2.
Lahore, History, Hc5.
Lake dwellings, N.
Lake Nyassa, History, Ho7.
Lakes, Landscape Gardening, Ag7.
Lakes, Physical Geography, Ng9.
Lamentations, Bible, T2.
Lampoons, Lp.
Lamps, Pc9.
Lancaster, History, Hc1.
Land, Law, Jp.
Land, Political Economy, Se2.
Land drainage, Agriculture, Af1.
Land drainage, Engineering, Ue8.
Landlord and Tenant, Law, Jp.
Landlord and Tenant, Political
    Economy, Se2.
Landscape Drawing, Fd1.
Landscape Gardening, Ag6.
Landscape Painting, Fd1.
Language, Ek.
Lansing, Michigan, U. S. Hu9.
Lapland, History, Hd9.
Lapland Voyages and Travels, Vd.

La Plata River, Va8.
Larynx, Diseases of, M3.
Lathe Work, Ub3.
Latin Language, Ek8.
Latin Literature, L7.
Latin Mythology, Tn6.
Latin Poetry, Lp7.
Latitude, Navigation, Cn5.
Latter Day Saints, Tc8.
Latvia, History, Hg3.
Laughter, Ethics, Ep4.
Laughter, Wit and Humor, Lw.
Laundry, D1.
Law, J.
Law, Ethics, Ep5.
Law of Nations, Jn.
Lawn-tennis, Fs8.
Lawns, Ag6.
Laxatives, M3.
Lead, Chemistry, Pc.
Lead, Geology, Ng6.
Lead, Manufacture, Um.
Lead, Metallurgy, Ue9.
Lead, Mining, Ue9.
Lead, Poison, M7.
Learning, Education, E.
Leases, Law, Js.
Leather, Ut6.
Leather Work, Ut6.
Leaves, Nh2.
Lectern, T8.
Lectures, Lo5.
Leeches, Medicine, M3.
Leeds, England, Hb1.
Leeward Islands, History, Ha6.

Lisbon, History, Hs1.

Litanies, T8.

Litany, Episcopal, Tc3.

Litany, Roman Catholic, Tc2.

Literary Criticisms, Lb3.

Literary History, L3-9.

Literary Men, Lives, B.

Literary Property, Jn.

Literary Societies, E9.

Literature, L.

Literature, Victorian, L4.

Lithography, Fp7.

Lithology, Ng3.

Lithuania, History, Hr1.

Liturgies, T8.

Liu-Kiu Islands, Hc1.

Live Stock, A4.

Liver, M3.

Liverpool, History, Hc1.

Lives, Biography, B.

Livonia, History, Hr1.

Lizards, Nh6.

Loadstone, Geology, Ng.

Loadstone, Magnetic, Pe1.

Loan Associations, Se9.

Loans, Banking, Se8.

Loans, National, Se7.

Lobsters, Nh6.

Local Governments, Sg. See Under Departments.

Lockjaw, M3.

Lockouts, Se4.

Locks, Ut2.

Locomotion, Animal, Nh3.

Locomotion, Disease, M3.

Locomotion, Physiology, Ma2.

Locomotives, Commerce, C2.

Locomotives, Engineering, Ue5.

Locomotor Ataxia, Disease, M5.

Locusts, Af8.

Logarithms, Pm3.

Logic, Ep3.

Loire, History, Hf1.

Lombardy, History, H1.

London, England, Hb1.

Long Island, New York U. S. Hu9.

Longevity, Mh2.

Longitude, Navigation, Cn5.

Loo-choo Islands, Hc1.

Looking Glasses, P2.

Loom, Um8.

Lord's Day, T8.

Lord's Prayer, T5.

Lord's Supper, T8.

Lorraine, History, Hf6.

Lotteries, Ep5.

Lotus, Religion, Tn4.

Louisiana, U. S. Hu9.

Louisville, Kentucky, U. S. Hu9.

Love, Ethics, Ep4.

Love, Sociology, S7.

Lower California, History, Ha5.

Lower California, Travels, Va5.

Loyalty, Ep5.

Loyalty Islands, History, Hc3.

Lubeck, History, Hg1.

Lubrication, Chemistry, Pc9.

Lubrication, Engineering, Ue3.

Lucknow, History, Hc5.

Luke, Bible, T2.

Lumber, Building Material, Ub4.

Lumber, Manufacture, Um.

Lumber, Trees, Af9.

Lunacy, M6.

Lunar, Tables, Na1.

Lungs, Me5.

Lusitania, History, Hs4.

Lute, Fm8.

Lutheran Church, Tc6.

Luxemburg, Hg1.

Luxor, History, He.

Luxury, Medical, Mf9.

Lycantrophy, Ep9.

Lyceums, E9.

Lying, Ep5.

Lymphatic Disease, M3.

Lynch Law, Jt.

Lyric Poetry, English, Lp2.

Lyric Poetry, Greek, Lp7.

Lyric Poetry, Latin, Lp7.

—M—

Maccabees, Bible, T2.

Maccabees, Knights of, H9.

Macedonia, History, Hk5.

Machine Construction, Ue3.

Machine Design, Ue3.

Machine Drawing, Fd3.

Machine Shop Practice, Ue2.

Machinery, Agricultural, A2.

Machinery, Electric, Pe4.

Machinery, Engineering, Ue3.

Machinery, Handbooks, Ue3.

MacKinley Mount, History, Ha3.

Madagascar, History, Ho8.

Maderia, History, Hs7.

Madison, Wisconsin, U. S. Hu9.

Madness, Insanity, M6.

Madness, Ethics, Ep3.

Madonna, Tc.

Madras, History, Hc5.

Madrid, History, Hs.

Madrigal, Music, Fm3.

Magazines, Gm4.

Magdalena River, Va8.

Magellan Straits of, Ha8.

Magic, Ep9.

Magic and Conjuring, Fs5.

Magic Lantern, P2.

Magistrates, Law, Jp.

Magistrates, Lives, B.

Magna Charta, Hb.

Magnet Electro, Pe.

Magnetic Needle, Cn5.

Magnetism, Animal, Ep9.

Magnetism, Electric, Pe1.

Magnetism, Human, Ep9.

Magyar, History, Hg3.

Magyar, Language, Ek9.

Mah-Jong Game, Fs3.

Mahomedanism, Tn3.

Mail, C5.

Maine, France, Hf1.

Maine, U. S. Hu9.

Maize, Af2.

Majolica, Fc.

Make up, Art of, Fs2.

Malabar Coast, History, Hc5.

Malacca, History, Hc4.

Malachi, Bible, T2.

Malacology, Nh6.

Malaga, History, Hs1.

Malarial, Mh.

Malarial Fever, M3.

Malaysia, History, Hc3.

Malpractice, Law, Js.

Malt, Db.

Malta Island, History, Hi2.

Malta, Knights of, H9.

Mamelukes, History, He1.

Mammals, Nh8.

Mammoth Cave, Kentucky, U. S. Hu9.

Man, Archæology, N2.

Man, Ethics, Ep3.

Man, Evolution, Mb.

Man, Isle of, Hb4.

Man, Natural History, N2.

Man, Physiology, Ma2.

Management, Business, Eb1.

Manasses, Prayer of, Bible, T2.

Manchester, England, Hb1.

Manchuria, History, Hc.

Mandamus, Js.

Mandolin, Fm8.

Manitoba, History, Ha2.

Manly Exercise, Mp.

Manners, E7.

Manners and Customs, H8.

Manometer, P5.

Manual Training, E3.

Manufacture, Um.

Manufacture, Chemistry of, Pc9.

Manures, Af1.

Manuscripts, G9.

Map Drawing, Fd3.

Maps, V1.

Maps, Astronomical, Na6.

Marble, Building, Ub1.

Marble, Sculpture, Fd7.

Marbling, Painting, Ub6.

Marbling, Paper Work, Fd8.

Marine Architecture, Cs.

Marine Engineering, Ue4.

Marine Insurance, C8.

Marine, Law, Js.

Marine, Plants, Nh6.

Marine, Surveying, Na8.

Marine, Zoology, Nh6.

Mariner's Compass, Cn5.

Mariolatry, T5.

Maritime Law, Jn.

Maritime Surveying, Na8.

Mark, Bible, T2.

Market Gardening, Ag1.

Marne, History, Hf1.

Maroons, History, Ha8.

Marquesas Islands, Hc3.

Marquetry, Fa6.

Marriage, Customs, H8.

Marriage, Ethics, Ep6.

Marriage, Law, Jp.

Marriage, Sacrament, T8.

Marriage, Sexual Science, Mg5.

Marriage, Social Science, S7.

Mars, Planet, Na2.

Marseilles, History, Hf1.

Marshall Islands, History, Hc2.

Martial Law, Jm.

Martinique, History, Ha6.

Martyrs, Christian, Tc.

Mary, Virgin, T5.

Maryland, U. S. Hu9.

Masks, Face, Dc3.

Masks, Plays, Lp2.

Masonry. Ub1.

Masons, F. & A. M., H9.

Masquerades, Fs4.

Masques, Dc3.

Mass, Tc2.

Massachusetts, U. S. Hu9.

Massage, M9.

Masses, Music, Fm5.

Master and Servant, Ep6.

Masts, Cs.

Matches, Pc9.

Materia Medica, M3.

Materialism, Ep2.

Materials, Strength of, Ue6.

Maternity, Mg3.

Mathematical Drawing, Fd3.

Mathematical Instruments, Pm.

Mathematics, Pm.

Mathematics, Engineering, Pm9.

Mathematics, Shop, Pm9.

Mathematics, Technical, Pm9.

Matins, T8.

Matrimony, Customs, H8.

Matrimony, Ethics, Ep6.

Matrimony, Social Science, S7.

Mats, Um8.

Matter, Philosophy, Ep2.

Matter, Physics, P.

Matthew, Bible, T2.

Maritus, History, Ho8.

Mauritania, History, Ho3.

Mausoleums, Fd7.

Maxims, L2.

Mayan Indians, Ha5.

McKinley, Mount, History, Ha3.

Meals, D2.

Measles, Disease, M3.

Measures, Pm5.

Meat, Mf.

Mecca, History, Hc7.

Mechanic Arts, U.

Mechanical Drawing, Fd3.

Mechanical Engineering, Ue1.

Mechanics, P3.

Mecklenberg, History, Hg1.

Medals, Fe5.

Media, History, Hc6.

Medical Botany, M3.

Medical Chemistry, Pc7.

Medical Education, M.

Medical Electricity, Pe9.

Medical Essays, M.

Medical Jurisprudence, Js.

Medical Schools, M.

Medicine, M.

Medicine, Practice of, M3.

Medieval Art, F9.

Medieval History, H3.

Meditations, T8.

Mediterranean, Voyages and Travels, Vm.

Melanesia, History, Hc3.

Melbourne, History, Hc3.

Melody, Music, Fm.

Memoirs, B.

Memorial Day, H8.

Memory, E6.

Memphis, Tenn., U. S. Hu9.

Menageries, Nh3.

Mendicity, S4.

Menonnites, Tc8.

Mensuration, Pm5.

Mental Aberration, M6.

Mental Arithmetic, Pm1.

Mental Diseases, M5.

Mental Healing, Ep9.

Mental Philosophy, Ep3.

Mental Physiology, Ep2.

Mental Suggestion, Ep9.

Menticulture, E6.

Mercantile Law, Js.

Merchandise, G.

Merchandise Commerce, C.

Merchandising Business, Eb7.

Merchants' Lives, B.

Mercury, Astronomy, Na2.

Mercury, Chemistry, Pc5.

Mercury, Metallurgy, Ue9.

Mesmerism, Ep9.

Mesopotamia, History, Hc7.

Messiah, T5.

Messiah, Music, Fm3.

Metal Roofing, Ub5.

Metal work, Art, Fd6.

Metal work, Manufactures, Um1.

Metallurgy, Ue9.

Metals, Brass, Etc., Um2.

Metals, Steel, Um1.

Metaphor, Ek2.

Metaphysics, Ep2.

Metempsychosis, Ep2.

Meteorites, Ng.

Meterology, Ng7.

Meteors, Na2.

Methodist Episcopal Church, Tc4.

Methodology, Logic, Ep3.

Metric System, Pm5.

Metrology, Pm5.

Metz, History, Hf1.

Meuse, History, Hf1.

Mexican Archæology, Ha5.

Mexicans, Indians, Ha5.

Mexican War, U. S. Hu5.

Mexico, History, Ha5.

Mexico, Voyages and Travels, Va5.

Micah, Bible, T2.

Michigan, U. S. Hu9.

Microbes, M2.

Micronesia, History, Hc2.

Microphone, Pe8.

Microphotography, Fp9.

Microscope, Nh5.

Middle Ages, H3.

Middlesex, England, Hb1.

Middlesex, Massachusetts, U. S. Hu9.

Midwifery, Mg.

Milan, History, Hi1.

Military Academies, Cm.

Military Architecture, Cm9.

Military Art and Science, Cm.

Military Biography, B.

Military Education, Cm.

Military Engineering, Cm1.

Military History, Cm.

Military Hygiene, Mh1.

Military Law, Jm.

Military Regulations, Cm1.

Military Schools, Cm.

Military Surgery, Ms.

Military Tactics, Cm1.

Militia, Cm1.

Milk, A5.

Millennium, T6.

Millerites, Tc7.

Millinery, Dc4.

Milling Machine, Ue3.

Mills, Ue2.

Milwaukee, Wisconsin, U. S. Hu9.

Mind and Body, Ep3.

Mind Cure, Ep9.

Mind reading, Ep9.

Mineralogy, Ng6.

Mines and Mining, Ue9.

Miniature Painting, Fd1.

Mining, Ue9.

Ministers' Lives, B.

Minneapolis, Minn., U. S. Hu9.

Minnesingers, Lp6.

Minnesota, U. S., Hu9.

Minorities, Sp.

Minstrels, Lp2.

Mints, Se7.

Miracle Plays, Lp2.

Miracles, T5.

Miracles, Fakes, Fs2.

Mirrors, P2.

Missals, Tc1.

Missionaries' Lives, B.

Missions, Tc9.

Mississippi, U. S., Hu9.

Missouri, U. S., Hu9.

Molecules, Zoology, Nh5.

Mistakes, Etiquette, E7.

Mistakes, Language. See countries.

Mites, Nh4.

Mnemonics, E6.

Moab, Bible, T2.

Mobs, Jt.

Model Making, Ue2.

Modelling, Fd7.

Modena, History, Hi1.

Modern History, H3.

Modesty, Ep6.

Modoc Indians, Hu1.

Moesia, History, Hg6.

Mohammedanism, Tn3.

Mohican Indians, Hu1.

Molasses, Pc9.

Moldavia, History, Hg4.

Molding, Ue2.

Molecules, Chemistry, Pc.

Moles, Nh3.

Mollusks, Nh6.

Molly Maguires, H9.

Moluccas, History, He3.

Monaco, History, Hf1.

Monarchy, Sp1.

Monasteries, Architecture, Fa2.

Monasteries, Theology, Tc1.

Monasticism, Tc2.

Money, Se7.

Mongolia, History, He.

Monkeys, Nh8.

Monks, Tc1.

Monmouth, England, Hb1.

Monograms, Fd9.

Monoplane, P9.

Monopolies, Se1.

Monotheism, T5.

Monroe Doctrine, Sp3.

Monstrosities, Animal, Nh3.

Monstrosities, Human, N2.

Montana, U. S. Hu9.

Monte Carlo, History, Hf1.

Montenegro, History, Hg6.

Months, Na9.

Montreal, Canada, Ha2.

Montserrat, History, Ha6.

Monuments, Fd7.

Moon, Na1.

Moot Courts, Jt.

Moraines, Ng2.

Moral Education, T.

Moral Philosophy, En5.

Morality Plays, Lp2.

Moravia, History, Hg4.

Moravians, Tc6.

Mormonism, Tn4.

Morocco, History, Ho8.

Morocco, Voyages and Travels, Vo3.

Moros, History, Hc2.

Morphia, M7.

Morphology, Animal, Nh3.

Morphology, Plants, Nh1.

Morristown, New Jersey, U. S. Hu9.

Mortality, Mh9.

Mortar, Ub2.

Mortgages, Law, Jp.

Mosaics, Fd4.

Mosaism, T1.

Mosavarians, Tc6.

Moselle, History, Hf1.

Moslems, Tn3.

Mosques, Fa2.

Mosquitoes, Nh4.

Mosses, Algæ, Nh6.

Mosses, Botany, Nh1.

Mother, Maternity, Mg3.

Mother, Philosophy, Ep6.

Moths, Nh4.

Motion, Anatomy, Ma.

Motion, Astronomy, Na.

Motion, Botany, Nh1.

Motion, Mechanics, P3.

Motion, Philosophy, Ep2.

Motion, Pictures, Fp4.

Motion, Physics, P3.

Motographs, Pe8.

Motor Boats, Construction, Cs7.

Motorcycle, Ut5.

Motors, Electric, Pe4.

Motors, Steam, Ue1.

Mottoes, Lq.

Mould, Nh1.

Moulding, Casting, Ue2.

Mouldings, Wood, Ub4.

Mound builders, Archæology, N.

Mound builders, Indians, U. S. Hu1.

Mounds, N.

Mount Vernon, New York, U. S. Hu9.

Mount Vernon, Virginia, U. S. Hu9.

Mountaineering, Fs9.

Mountains, Ng8.

Mouth, Disease, M3.

Mouth, Surgery, Ms1.

Moving Pictures, Fp4.

Mozambique, History, Ho4.

Muck, Agriculture, Af1.

Mulberry, A7.

Mule, Nh8.

Mummies, H8.

Mumps, Disease, M3.

Munich, History, Hg5.

Municipal Corporations, Sg.

Municipal Government, Sg.

Municipal Law, Sg.

Munitions, Cm.

Mural Decoration, Fd4.

Murder, Jt.
Muscat, History, Hc7.
Muscle, Disease of, M3.
Museums, F8.
Mushrooms, Ag.
Music, Fm.
Music, Acoustics, P1.
Music, Essays, Fm.
Music, History, Fm9.
Music, Instruction Books, Fm2.
Music, Sacred, Fm5.
Music, Score, Fm4.
Music, Theory, Fm.
Music, Vocal, Fm3.
Musical Composition, Fm1.
Musical Dictionaries, Fm9.
Musical Education, Fm2.
Musical Instruments, Fm8.
Musicians' Lives, B.
Mussels, Nh6.
Mustard, Af6.
Mutiny, Jn.

Mutual Benefit Societies, S9.
Mycenæ, History, Hk5.
Mycology, Nh1.
Myopia, Me2.
Mysore, History, Hc5.
Mysteries, Ep9.
Mystery Plays, Lp2.
Mysticism, Tc8.
Mythology, American, Tn9.
Mythology, England, Tn9.
Mythology, Egypt, Tn8.
Mythology, General, Tn5.
Mythology, Greek, Tn6.
Mythology, Indian, Tn9.
Mythology, Norse, Tn7.
Mythology, Oriental, Tn8.
Mythology, Roman, Tn6.
Mythology, Russian, Tn8.
Mythology, Scotland, Tn9.
Mythology, Teutonic, Tn7.
Myths, Tn5.

—N—

Nahum, Bible, T2.
Nails, Manufacture, Um1.
Names, Geographical, Bc8.
Names, Persons, Bc8.
Nantucket, Massachusetts, U. S. Hu9.
Naples, History, Hi1.
Narcotics, M7.
Nasal passages, Me4.
Natal, History, Ho7.
National Banks, Se8.
National Law, Jn.
National Songs, Fm3.
Nationalism, Se5.
Nations, Law of, Jn.
Natural History, Nh.
Natural History of Man, Ng4.
Natural Philosophy, P1.

Natural Religion, Tc1.
Natural Science, P1.
Natural Selection, Mb.
Natural Theology, Tc1.
Naturalists' Lives, B.
Naturalization, Se3.
Nature, Nh.
Nature, Ethics, Ep2.
Nature, Study, Nh9.
Nautical Almanacs, Gr1.
Nautical Astronomy, Na8.
Navajo, Indians, Hu1.
Naval Academies, Cn.
Naval Architecture, Cn9.
Naval Art and Science, Cn.
Naval Artillery, Cn1.
Naval Battles, Cn.
Naval Biography, B.

Naval History, Cn.
Naval Hygiene, Mh1.
Naval Life, Cn.
Naval Surgery, Ms.
Naval Tactics, Cn1.
Naval Warfare, Cn1.
Navigation, Cn5.
Navigation, Astronomy, Na8.
Navigator's Island, Hc2.
Navy, Cn.
Nebraska, U. S., Hu9.
Nebulae, Na1.
Necessity, Ep2.
Neck, Surgery, Ms.
Necromancy, Ep9.
Necrosis, Disease, M3.
Needlework, Dc5.
Negroes, Ethnology, N2.
Negroes, Slavery, S6.
Nehemiah, Bible, T2.
Neolithic Age, N.
Nepaul, History, Hc5.
Nerves, M5.
Nervous System, M5.
Nestorians, Tc2.
Netherlands, History, Hg9.
Netherlands, Voyages and Travels, Vg9.
Neupommern, Hc3.
Neuralgia, M3.
Neuritis, M3.
Neurology, M5.
Neurosis, Disease, M3.
Neutrality, Jn.
Nevada, U. S. Hu9.
New Britain (Neupommern), History, Hc3.
New Britain, Connecticut, U. S. Hu9.
New Brunswick, Canada, History, Ha2.
New Brunswick, N. J., U. S. Hu9.
New Caledonia, History, Hc3.

New Church, Tc7.
New England States, U. S. Hu9.
New England States, Early History, Hu2.
New Foundland, History, Ha2.
New France, History, Ha2.
New Guinea, Hc3.
New Hampshire, U. S. Hu9.
New Haven, Connecticut, U. S. Hu9.
New Hebrides, History, Hc3.
New Holland, History, Hc3.
New Jersey, U. S. Hu9.
New Jerusalem, Religion, Tc7.
New London, Connecticut, U. S. Hu9.
New Mexico, U. S. Hu9.
New Orleans, Louisiana, U. S., Hu9.
New South Wales, History, Hc3.
New Testament, T2.
New Year, H8.
NewYork City, New York, U. S. Hu9.
New York State, U. S. Hu9.
New Zealand, History, Hc3.
Newark, New Jersey, U. S. Hu9.
Newburgh, New York, U. S. Hu9.
Newport, Rhode Island, U. S. Hu9.
Newspapers, Daily, Gm5.
Newspapers, Weekly, Gm6.
Newspapers, Criticism, Lb3.
Newspapers, Journalism, Lb2.
Niagara Falls, Canada, Ha2.
Niagara Falls, United States, Hu9.
Nicaragua, History, Ha4.
Nicene Creed, T8.
Nichiremism, Tn1.
Nickel, Coinage, Se7.
Nickel, Ores, Ng6.
Nicknames, G2.
Niger River, History, Ho4.

Nightmare, Ep9.

Nihilism, Se5.

Nile, He.

Ninevah, History, Hc7.

Nobility, Bc2.

Nocturne, Music, Fm4.

Noise, P1.

Nom de Plume, G2.

Non Christian Religions, Tn.

Nonconformists, Tc3.

Nonjurors, Tc.

Nonresistance, Ep5.

Norfolk, England, Hb1.

Norfolk, Virginia, U. S. Hu9.

Norfolk Islands, History, Hc2.

Normal Schools, E1.

Normandy, History, Hf1.

Normans, History, Hb1.

Norse Mythology, Tn7.

North Africa, History, Ho3.

North American Indians, Hu1.

North Carolina, U. S. Hu9.

North Dakota, U. S. Hu9.

North Pole, Hn.

North Pole, Voyages and Travels, Vn.

Northampton, England, History, Hb1.

Northampton, Massachusetts, U. S. Hu9.

Northeast Boundary of the, U. S. Hu5.

Northeast Passage, Hn1.

Northeast Passage, Voyages and Travels, Vn1.

Northern Lights, Na.

Northmen in America, Ha.

Northwest Boundary of the U. S. Hu5.

Northwest Passage, Hn1.

Northwest Passage, Voyages and Travels, Vn1.

Norwalk, Connecticut, U. S. Hu9.

Norway, Army and Navy, Hd5.

Norway, History, Hd3.

Norway, Separate Places, Hd4.

Norway, Voyages and Travels, Vd.

Norwegian, Language, Ek5.

Norwegian, Literature, L6.

Nose, Me4.

Nottingham, England, History, Hc1.

Nova Scotia, History, Ha2.

Novelists' Lives, B.

Novels, Entered under title only.

Nubia, History, He.

Nuisance, Hygiene, Mhl.

Nuisance, Law, Jp.

Nullification, Law, Jn.

Numbers, Arithmetic, Pm3.

Numbers, Book of, Bible, T2.

Numismatics, Fe5.

Nunneries, Tc1.

Nuns, Tc1.

Nuremberg, History, Hg5.

Nurses and Nursing, M8.

Nutrition, Mf1.

Nyassa Lake, Ho7.

Nyassaland, History, Ho5.

—O—

Oaths, Ethics, Ep5.

Oaths, Law, Jp.

Obadiah, Bible, T2.

Obelisks, Fd7.

Obesity, Mf9.

Object Teaching, E3.

Obstetrics, Mg2.

Occult Sciences, Ep9.

Ocean, Physical Geography, Ng9.
Ocean, Zoology, Nh6.
Oceanica, History, Hc2.
Oceanica, Voyages and Travels, Vc2.
Odd Fellows, H9.
Odes, English, Lp2.
Odontology, Ms7.
Odontology, Animal, Nh3.
Oesophagus, Disease, M3.
Offertory, Music, Fm5.
Office Management, Eb1.
Office, Tenure, of, Sp.
Ohio, U. S., Hu9.
Oil, Chemistry, Pc9.
Oil, Manufacture, Um6.
Oil, Mining, Ue9.
Oil Engines, Ue3.
Oil Painting, Fd1.
Oise, France, Hf1.
Oklahoma, U. S. Hu9.
Old Age, Mh2.
Old Books, G9.
Old Testament, Bible, T2.
Olfaction, Ep2.
Olfaction, Physiology, Ma2.
Oligarchy, Sp.
Olives, Ag3.
Oman, History, Hc7.
Omens, Ep.
Omnipotence, God, T5.
Ontario, Canada, Ha2.
Ontology, Ep2.
Oology, Nh7.
Opal, Geology, Ng6.
Opal, Jewelry, Fe7.
Opera, Books about, Fm6.
Opera, Music, Fm3.
Opera, Score, Fm4.
Operetta, Music, Fm3.
Operetta, Score, Fm4.
Operetta, Stories of, Fm6.
Opthalmia, Me2.

Opium, M7.
Optic Nerve, Me2.
Optical Instruments, P2.
Optics, P2.
Optimism, Ep2.
Oracles, Ep9.
Orange, New Jersey, U. S. Hu9.
Orange Free States, History, Ho8.
Oranges, Ag3.
Orations, Collections, Lo6.
Orations, Individual, Lo5.
Oratories, Books About, Fm6.
Oratories, Music, Fm3.
Oratories, Score, Fm4.
Orators, Lives, B.
Oratory, Lo.
Orbit, Astronomy,Comets, Na2.
Orbit, Astronomy, Moon, Na1.
Orchards, Ag4.
Orchestral Music, Fm1.
Orchids, Ag5.
Orders, Architecture, Fa.
Orders, Heraldry, Bc2.
Orders, Knighthood, Bc2.
Orders, Ministry, T8.
Orders, Monastic, Tc1.
Orders, Sacraments, T8.
Ordination, T8.
Ordinance, Cm1.
Oregon, U. S. Hu9.
Ores, Metallurgy, Ue9.
Ores, Mineralogy, Ng6.
Organ, Fm8.
Organ,Music, Fm4.
Organic Chemistry, Pc6.
Oriental Language, Ek9.
Oriental Literature, L8.
Origin of Species, Mb.
Original Sin, T6.
Orinoco River, Va8.
Orleans, France, Hf1.
Ornament, Fd4.
Ornamental Alphabets, Fd9.

Ornamental Gardening, Ag6.

Ornaments, Toilet, Dc8.

Ornithology, Nh7.

Orphans, Ethics, Ep6.

Orphans, Law, Jp.

Orthodoxy, Tc1.

Orthœpy, Ek3.

Orthographic Projection, Pm4.

Orthography, Ek2.

Orthopedics, Ms.

Osteology, Animal, Nh3.

Osteology, Human, Ma1.

Oswego, New York, U. S. Hu9.

Otaheite, History, Hc2.

Ottoman Empire, Ho.

Oudh, History, Hc5.

Outdoor, Life, Fsl.

Ownership, Se2.

Overtures, Music, Fm4.

Ox, A4.

Oxford, England, History, Hf1.

Oxford Movement, Tc3.

Oxygen, Chemistry, Pc5.

Oxygen, Uses, M3.

Oyster, Nh6.

—P—

Pacific Ocean, Ng9.

Padua, Italy, Hil.

Paganism, Tn.

Pageants, H8.

Pain, Ethics, Ep9.

Pain, Physical, M.

Paint, Chemistry, Pc9.

Paint, Manufacture, Um6.

Painted Glass, Fc.

Painters' Lives, F3.

Painting, Fd.

Painting, Fine Art, Fd1.

Painting, Sign, Ub6.

Painting, Useful Arts, Ub6.

Paintings, F8.

Palaces, Fa4.

Palatinate, Germany, Hg1.

Paleography, Fe3.

Paleontology, Ng3.

Palestine, Hc7.

Palestine, Voyages and Travels, Vc7.

Palmistry, Ep7.

Palmyra, History, Hc7.

Palsy, M3.

Pamphlets, Gp.

Panama, History, Ha8.

Pancreas, Disease, M3.

Panics, Se8.

Pantheism, Philosophy, Ep3.

Pantheism, Theology, Tn1.

Panther, Nh8.

Pantomime, Fs4.

Papacy, Tc2.

Papal States, Hil.

Paper Manufactures, Um3.

Paper Hanging, Ub7.

Paper Money, Se7.

Papuans, History, Hc3.

Papyrus, G9.

Parables, Bible, T2.

Parables, Literature, La.

Parabola, Pm4.

Parades, H8.

Paradise, T6.

Paraguay, History, Ha8.

Paralysis, M3.

Parasites, Animal, Nh3.

Parasites, Disease, M2.

Parasites, Plants, Nh1.

Parents, Ep6.

Paris, France, Hf1.

Parks, Ag6.
Parliament, Sp4.
Parliamentary Practice, Jr.
Parlor Games, Fs4.
Parody, Lp.
Parquetry, Ub4.
Parrots, Nh7.
Parseeism, Tn4.
Parthia, History, Hc6.
Parties, Fs4.
Partnership, Contracts, Jp.
Partnership, Corporation, Se1.
Passaic, New Jersey, U. S. Hu9.
Passamaquoddy Indians, Hu1.
Passionists, Tc2.
Passion Play, Lp2.
Passions, Ep4.
Passover, Jews, Hc8.
Passover, Lord's Supper, T8.
Pastoral Poetry, Lp2.
Pastoral Theology, T7.
Pastry, D3.
Patagonia, History, Ha8.
Patent Law, Jn.
Patents, U3.
Paterson, New Jersey, U. S., Hu9.
Pathology, M3.
Patience, Cards, Fs3.
Patience,Ethics, Ep6.
Patriarchs, Br.
Patriotism, Ep5.
Patriots, Br.
Patrons of Husbandry, Sp.
Pattern Making, Ue2.
Pauperism, S4.
Pavements, Ue6.
Pawnbroking, Se9.
Pawnee Indians, Hu1.
Peace, Ethics, Ep5.
Peace Treaty, Hague, Sp.
Peaches, Ag4.
Pearls, Fe7.
Pears, Ag4.

Peasantry, Country Life, A9.
Peasantry, Labor, Se3.
Peat, Uf.
Pedagogics, E3.
Pedestrianism, Fs1.
Pedigrees, Bc3.
Peerage, Bc2.
Peking, History, Hc.
Peloponnesian War, Hk5.
Pen Drawing, Fd2.
Penal Institutions, S3.
Penance, T8.
Pendulum, Ut3.
Penitence, T6.
Penitentiaries, S3.
Penmanship, Ek2.
Pennsylvania, U. S. Hu9.
Penobscot Indians, Hu1.
Penology, Jt.
Pensions, Sp.
Pentateuch, Bible, T2.
Peoria, Illinois, U. S. Hu9.
Pepper, Af6.
Pequot Indians, Hu1.
Perception, Ethics, Ep2.
Perennials, Ag5.
Perfection, Ethics, Ep6.
Perfumery, Chemistry, Pc9.
Perfumery, Toilet, Dc8.
Periodicals, Gm7 to 9.
Peritonitis, Disease, M3.
Perpetual Motion, P3.
Persecution, Tc.
Persepolis, History, Hc6.
Persia, Hc6.
Persia, Voyages and Travels, Vc6.
Persian Language, Ek9.
Persian Literature, L8.
Persian Wars, Hk5.
Personal Liberty, Ethics, Ep2.
Personal Liberty, Political Science, Sp.
Personal Property, Law, Jp.

Personal Tax, Federal, Se2.
Personal Tax, Local, Sg.
Personality, Ethics, Ep5.
Perspective, Fd1.
Perspective, Linear, Fd5.
Peru, History, Ha8.
Pessimism, Ep2.
Pests, Af8.
Peter, Bible, T2.
Petrifaction, Ng3.
Petrograd, History, Hr1.
Petrography, Ng.
Petroleum, Chemistry, Pc9.
Petroleum, Mining, Ue9.
Petrology, Ng.
Pets, A3.
Pewter, Fd6.
Phallisms, Tn4.
Phanerogams, Nh1.
Phantoms, Ep9.
Pharmacy, M1.
Pheasants, Nh7.
Philadelphia, Pennsylvania, U. S. Hu9.
Philanthropists' Lives, B.
Philanthropy, Ep6.
Philately, Fe6.
Philemon, Bible, T2.
Philippians, Bible, T2.
Philippines, History, Hc2.
Philippines, Voyages and Travels, Vc2.
Philistines, Hc7.
Philology, Ek1.
Philosophers' Lives, B.
Philosophical Instruments, P.
Philosophy, Ep.
Philosophy, Ancient, Ep1.
Philosophy, Critical, Ep.
Philosophy, Domestic, Ep6.
Philosophy, Moral, Ep5.
Philosophy, Natural, P1.
Philosophy of History, H7.

Phoenicia, History, Hc7.
Phonetics, Ek3.
Phonograph, P1.
Phonography, Eb2.
Phonology, Ek1.
Phosphates, Agriculture, Af1.
Phosphates, Chemistry, Pc9.
Phosphates, Mineralogy, Ng6.
Phosphorescence, P2.
Photochronography, Fp5.
Photo Electrotyping, Fp8.
Photo Engraving, Fp8.
Photographic Chemistry, Fp3.
Photographs, Animals, Fp5.
Photographs, Collections, Fp1.
Photographs, Supplies, Fp2.
Photography, Fp.
Photography, Color, Fp4.
Photography, Game, Fp5.
Photography, Special Processes, Fp4.
Photo-Lithography, Fp7.
Photomicrography, Fp9.
Photoplay, Fp4
Photo Zincography, Fp7.
Phrase Books, Ek3.
Phrenology, Ep8.
Phrygia, History, Hc7.
Phthisis, Disease, Me5.
Physic Research, Ep9.
Physical Culture, Mp.
Physical Geography, Ng8.
Physical Geology, Ng.
Physical Training, Mp.
Physicians' Lives, B.
Physics, P.
Physiognomy, Ep8.
Physiography, Ng8.
Physiological Chemistry, Pc7.
Physiology, Ma2.
Physiology, Ethics, Ep2.
Piano, Fm8.
Piano Score, Fm4.

Pictures, Exhibitions, F8.
Picturesque, F1.
Piers, Ue8.
Pig, A4.
Pigeons, A7.
Pigments, Chemistry, Pc9.
Pigments, Manufacture, Um6.
Pigmies, N2.
Piles, Disease, M3.
Pilgrim Fathers, Hu9.
Pilgrimage, T8.
Pilory, Jp.
Pipe Fitting, Uc9.
Pineapple, Af6.
Piquet, Cards, Fs3.
Piracy, Jt.
Pirates, V6.
Pisa, Italy, Hi1.
Pisciculture, Nh6.
Pistol, Ut2.
Pitcairn's Island, History, Hc2.
Pittsburgh, Pennsylvania, U. S.,
    Hu9.
Placers, Ng6.
Plague, Disease, M3.
Plague, Hygiene, Mh9.
Plan Printing, Fp.
Plan Reading, Ub.
Planets, Na2.
Plans, Building, Ub.
Planting, Af.
Plants, Botany, Nh1.
Plants, Gardens, Ag.
Plaster, Ub2.
Plastering, Ub2.
Plate, Glass, Um4.
Plate, Manufacture, Um1.
Plated Ware, Um1.
Plating, Electro, Pe2.
Platinum, Pc5.
Platonists, Ep1.
Players' Lives, B.
Playing Cards, Fs3.

Plays, Amateur, Lp4.
Plays, American, Lp2.
Plays, Criticisms, Lp1.
Plays, Collective, Lp3.
Plays, English, Lp2.
Plays, French, Lp5.
Plays, General Essays, Lp1.
Plays, Greek, Lp7.
Plays, Historical, Lp1.
Plays, Latin, Lp7.
Plays, Persian, Lp8.
Plays, Unclassified, Lp9.
Playwright, Jn.
Pleading, Jt.
Pleasure, Ep4.
Pleurisy, Disease, Me5.
Plow, A2.
Plumbing, Ub8.
Plurality of Worlds, Na.
Plymouth, Massachusetts, U. S.,
    Hu9.
Pneumatic Transmission, Ue.
Pneumatics, P5.
Pneumonia, Me5.
Poaching, Fs9.
Poetry, American, Lp2.
Poetry, Collective, Lp3.
Poetry, Criticism, Lp.
Poetry, English, Lp2.
Poetry, Essays, Lp.
Poetry, Individual, Lp2.
Poetry, Juvenile, Lp4.
Poets' Lives, B.
Poisons, M7.
Poker, Cards, Fs3.
Poland, History, Hr2.
Poland, Language, Ek9.
Poland, Literature, L9.
Polar Regions, Vn.
Polariscope, P2.
Police, Sg8.
Polish Language, Ek9.
Polish Literature, L9.

Polish Poetry, Lp9.

Polishing, Wood, Ub6.

Politeness, E7.

Political Economy, Se.

Political Parties, Sp2.

Politics, See Countries, Sp.

Pollution, Mh1.

Polo, Fs8.

Polygamy, Ethics, Ep6.

Polygamy, Law, Jp.

Polygamy, Mohammedanism, Tn3.

Polygamy, Mormonism, Tn4.

Polynesia, History, Hc2.

Polytechnic Schools, E3.

Polytheism, Tn4.

Pomerania, History, Hg1.

Pomology, Ag3.

Pompeii, History, Hi1.

Ponds, Ag6.

Pool, Fs3.

Poor, S4.

Poorhouses, S4.

Popes, History, Tc2.

Popes' Lives, Br.

Population, Se3.

Porcelain, Fc.

Porto Rico, History, Ha7.

Porto Rico, Voyages and Travels, Va6.

Portrait Painting, Fd1.

Portraits, Fd1.

Ports, Engineering, Ue6.

Portsmouth, England, Hb1.

Portugal, History, Hs4.

Portugal, Army and Navy, Ha6.

Portugal, Guide Books, Vs.

Portugal, Separate Places, Hs5.

Portuguese, East Africa, History, Ho4.

Portuguese Language, Ek7.

Portuguese Literature, L5.

Portuguese West Africa, Ho7.

Posen, History, Hg1.

Positivism, Ep2.

Posology, M3.

Possession, Law, Jp.

Post mortem Examinations, M3.

Post Office, C5.

Postage Stamps, Fe6.

Posters, Fd2.

Potato, Af2.

Potential, Pe.

Pottery, Fc.

Pottery Decoration, Fc1.

Pottery Manufacture, Um4.

Poultry, A7.

Poverty, S4.

Powder, Pc9.

Power, Ue1.

Powers, Sp.

Practical Theology, T9.

Prague, History, Hg3.

Prayer Meetings, Tc9.

Prayers, T8.

Preachers' Lives, Br.

Preaching, T7.

Precious Metals, Geology, Ng6.

Precious Metals, Metallurgy, Ue9.

Precious Stones, Geology, Ng6.

Precious Stones, Jewelry, Fe7.

Precious Stones, Mineralogy, Ng6.

Predestination, T6.

Predictions, Ep9.

Pre-existence, Ethics, Ep9.

Pre-existence, Theology, T6.

Prehistoric, Archæology, N.

Prehistoric, Man, N2.

Presages, Ep9.

Presbyterianism, Tc5.

Prescriptions, M1.

Preserving, D3.

Presidential Government, Sp2.

Presidents' Lives, B.

Press, Liberty of, Sp.

Press, Printing, Fd8.

Prestidigitation, Fs5.

Prices, Se.

Pride, Ethics, Ep4.

Priesthood, Tc2.

Priests, See Special Religions.

Priests' Lives, Br.

Primary Batteries, Pe2.

Primers, E3.

Primogeniture, Law, Jp.

Princes, Sp1.

Princeton, New Jersey, U. S. Hu9.

Principal and Agent, Jp.

Printing, Fd8.

Printing Inks, Um7.

Prints, Fe1.

Prisons, S3.

Private Judgment, Ja.

Private Schools, E1.

Private Theatricals, Lp4.

Privateers, Jn.

Privation, Mf9.

Prizes, Law, Jn.

Probabilities, Pm8.

Probate, Js.

Probation, T6.

Procedure, Jt.

Process Work, Fp8.

Processions, H8.

Products of a Temperate Clime, Af2.

Profanity, Ethics, Ep5.

Profanity, Law, Jp.

Profit Sharing, Se4.

Progress, H7.

Progress, Political, Se1.

Prohibited Books, G8.

Prohibition, Ethics, Ep4.

Prohibition, Temperance, M7.

Projectiles, Military Science, Cm1.

Projectiles, Naval Science, Cn1.

Projecting, P2.

Projection, Fd3.

Pronunciation, Ek3.

Proof, Law, Jp.

Proof-reading, Ek2.

Propellers, Ue4.

Proper Names, Bc8.

Property, Law, Jp.

Property, Political Science, Se2.

Prophecy, T3.

Prophets, T3.

Prose, English, Ek4.

Prose, Greek, Ek8.

Prose, Latin, Ek8.

Prose, Rhetoric, Ek2.

Prosody, English, Ek4.

Prosody, Greek, Ek8.

Prosody, Latin, Ek8.

Prosody, Philology, Ek1.

Prostitution, Ethics, Ep5.

Prostitution, Law, Jp.

Protection, Se.

Protestant Episcopal Church, Tc3.

Protestantism, Tc3.

Protoplasm, Mb.

Protozoa, Nh6.

Provence, History, Hf1.

Proverbs, Lq.

Proverbs, Bible, T2.

Providence, Rhode Island, U. S. Hu9.

Provincialism, Ek4.

Pruning, Ag3.

Prussia, History, Hg.

Psalmody, Music, Fm5.

Psalms, Bible, T2.

Psalter, T8.

Pseudonyms, G2.

Psychical Research, Ep9.

Psychoanalysis, Ep2.

Psychology, Ep2.

Psychology, Medical, M8.

Public Documents, R.

Public Health, Mh1.

Public Libraries, G4.

Public Schools, E1.

Publishers' Lives, B.

Real Presence, T8.
Real Property, Law, Js.
Realism, Ep2.
Reason, Philosophy, Ep3.
Reason, Theology, Tc1.
Rebellion, U. S., Hu6.
Rebellion, Political Science, Sp.
Receipts, Chemistry, Pc.
Receipts, Domestic Arts, D3.
Receipts, Medical, M.
Receipts, Useful Arts, U2.
Reciprocity, Se.
Recitations, Lr.
Recreations, Fs.
Recruiting, Cm.
Redemption, T6.
Referendum, Sp.
Reflection, Ethics, Ep3.
Reflection, Heat, P3.
Reflection, Light, P2.
Reflections, Drawing, Fd2.
Reform Schools, S3.
Reformation, Tc.
Reformatories, S3.
Reformers' Lives, B.
Refraction, Heat, P3.
Refraction, Light, P2.
Refrigeration, Chemistry, Pe.
Refrigeration, Machines, Ue3.
Regalia, Heraldry, Bc3-7.
Regalia, Religious, T9.
Regalia, Secret Societies, H9.
Regattas, Fs6.
Regeneration, T6.
Regimen, Mh.
Reign of Terror, Hf.
Reincarnation, Ep2.
Rejuvenation, M.
Relativity, Pm.
Relics, T.
Religion, T.
Religion and Science, Tc.
Religions, Christian, Tc.

Religions, Non Christian, Tn.
Religions, Philosophy, Ep5.
Religious Art, F5.
Religious Biography, Br.
Religious Biography, Collective, Br1.
Religious Ceremonies, T8.
Religious Education, T1.
Religious Essays, T.
Religious Festivals, T8.
Religious History, Tc.
Religious Liberty, Tc.
Religious Orders, Under Separate Religion.
Religious Philosophy, T.
Religious Poetry, T8.
Religious Services, T8.
Religious Theories, T.
Remedies, M3.
Renaissance, Architecture, Fa.
Renaissance, Fine Arts, F4.
Renaissance, History, H3.
Renaissance, Religions, Tc.
Rent, Political Economy, Se2.
Repentance, T6.
Reporting, Lb2.
Reports, Under Subjects, R.
Repouseé Work, Fd6.
Reptiles, Nh6.
Republican Party, Sp2.
Republics, Sp2.
Reservoirs, Ue8.
Residences, Architecture, Fa4.
Resins, Um5.
Resonators, P4.
Respiration, Me5.
Responsive Worship, T8.
Rest, Mh5.
Restoration, English, Hb.
Restoration, French, Hf.
Restoration, Jews, Tn2.
Resurrection, T5.
Retribution, T6.

Revelation, Bible, T2.
Revenue, Se7.
Revival of Letters, L.
Revivals, Te9.
Revolutionary War, U. S. Hu4.
Revolutions, Sp.
Rhaetia, History, Hg4.
Rheinish Bavaria, History, Hg5.
Rheinish Prussia, Hg.
Rhetoric, Ek2.
Rheumatism, M3.
Rhine Province, History, Hg1.
Rhodesia, History, Ho7.
Rhode Island, U. S. Hu9.
Rhodes, History, He7.
Rhyme, Ek4.
Rice, Af2.
Riches, Se.
Richmond, Virginia, U. S. Hu9.
Rickets, Disease, M3.
Riddles, Fs4.
Riding, Fs7.
Rifle, Ut2.
Rifle, Range, Cm1.
Rifle, Sports, Fs9.
Rigging, Ship, Cs.
Riggs Disease, Ms7.
Right and Wrong, Ep3.
Rights of Woman, S7.
Rings, Customs, H8.
Rings, Jewelry, Fe8.
Rio de Janerio, History, Ha6.
Riots, Jt.
Rites and Ceremonies, Church, T8.
Ritual, T8.
Ritualism, T8.
Riu-Kiu Islands, He1.
Rivers, Engineering, Ue8.
Rivers, Physical Geography, Ng9.
Rivers, Shipping, C1.
Rivets, Ue2.
Riviera History, Hi1.
Roads, Ue6.

Roads, Commerce, C.
Roads, Engineering, Ue6.
Robbery, Jt.
Rochester, New York, U. S. Hu9.
Rocks, Ng6.
Rocky Mountains, U. S. Hu9.
Rod, E3.
Rodentia, Nh3.
Roentgen Rays, Pe6.
Roman Architecture, Fa1.
Roman Catholic Church, T2.
Roman Law, Ja.
Roman Mythology, Tn6.
Romances, Fiction, L.
Romances, Poetry, Lp.
Romanism, Tc2.
Romans, Bible, T2.
Romans, Epistles to the Bible, T2.
Romanticism, L3.
Rome, Ancient, History, Hk.
Rome, Modern, History, Hi1.
Rome, Voyages and Travels, Vk.
Roofs, Ub5.
Rope Making, Um8.
Rosary, Catholic Church, Tc2.
Rosary, Prayers, T8.
Roses, Ag5.
Rosicrucians, H9.
Rotterdam, History, Hg9.
Roumania, History, Hg4.
Roumanian Language, Ek9.
Rowing, Fs6.
Royalty, Sp1.
Rubber Manufacture, Um5.
Rug Making, Um8.
Rugs, Furniture, D9.
Rulers' Lives, B
Rules of Order, Jr.
Rumania, History, Hg4.
Running, Fs1.
Rural Architecture, Fa4.
Rural Economy, A.
Rural Life, A9.

Russia, History, Hr.
Russia, Army and Navy, Hr7.
Russia, Separate Places, Hrl.
Russia, Voyages and Travels, Vr.
Russian Church, Tc2.
Russian Language, Ek9.

Russian Literature, L9.
Russo-Turkish War, Hr.
Ruth, Bible, T2.
Ruthenian Language, Ek9.
Ruthenians, History, Hg3.

—S—

Sabbath, T8.
Sacraments, T8.
Sacred Art, F5.
Sacred Drama, Lp2.
Sacred History, T.
Sacred Music, Fm5.
Sacred Poetry, Lp2.
Sacrifice, T8.
Sacrilege, T8.
Saddlery, Ut6.
Sago, Um5.
Safe Manufacture, Um1.
Safety Valve, Ue5.
Sagas, L9.
Sahara, History, Ho3.
Sailing, Fs6.
Sailing, Vessels, Cs3.
Sailors' Lives, B.
Sails, Cs.
Saint Helena Island, History, Ho6.
Saint John, Knights of, H9.
Saint Louis, Missouri, U. S. Hu9.
Saint Paul, Minnesota, U. S. Hu9.
Saint Petersburg, History, Hrl.
Saint Vitus Dance, M3.
Saints' Biography, Br.
Salamanca, History, Hsl.
Salads, D3.
Sale, Business, Eb.
Salem, Massachusetts, U. S. Hu9.
Salerno, History, Hi2.
Salesmanship, Eb7.
Salicylic Acid, Pc6.
Salt, Um5.

Salt Lake City, Utah, U. S. Hu9.
Salvador, History, Ha4.
Salvation, T6.
Salvation Army, Tc9.
Samoan Islands, History, Hc2.
Samuel, Bible, T2.
Sanctuary, J.
San Francisco, California, U. S. Hu9.
San Juan, Porto Rico, History, Ha7.
San Marino, History, Hi1.
San Salvador, History, Ha4.
Sanitary Science, Building, Ub9.
Sanitary Science, Engineering, Ue8.
Sanitary Science, Hygiene, Mh1.
Sanskrit Language, Ek9.
Sanskrit Literature, L9.
Santo Domingo, History, Ha6.
Saracens, History, Hc7.
Saratoga, New York, U. S. Hu9.
Sardinia, History, Hi2.
Sarmatia, History, Hr2.
Saskatchewan, History, Ha2.
Satan, T6.
Satire, Lw.
Saturn, Na2.
Savannah, Georgia, U. S. Hu9.
Saving Grace, T6.
Savings Bank, Se8.
Savoy, History, Hf.
Saws, Building Tools, Ub3.
Saws, Machine, Ue3.

Saxony, History, Hg.

Saxophone, Fm8.

Scalds, M8.

Scalp, Mh6.

Scandinavia, History, H2.

Scandinavian Architecture, Fa.

Scandinavian Language, Ek5.

Scandinavian Literature, L9.

Scandinavian Mythology, Tn7.

Scarlatina, M3.

Scarlet Fever, M3.

Scepticism, Tc1.

Scepticism, Ethics, Ep2.

Schleswig-Holstein, History, Hg1.

Scholastic Philosophy, Ep1.

School Books, E3.

School Houses, Architecture, Fa3.

School Hygiene, Mh1.

School Music, Fm2.

Schoolmasters, E.

Schools, E1.

Sciatica, Disease, M3.

Science and Religion, Tc.

Science, Mental, Ep3.

Science, Military, Cm1.

Science, Natural, P1.

Science, Naval, Cn1.

Scientific Associations, E9.

Scientific Education, E3.

Scientific Men, Lives, B.

Scientific Societies, E9.

Scilly Islands, History, Hb1.

Scorpions, Nh4.

Scotch Language, Ek9.

Scotch Presbyterians, Tc5.

Scotland, History, Hb4.

Scotland, Separate Places, Hb5.

Scotland, Voyages and Travels, Vb3.

Scottish Poetry, Authors, Lp2.

Scottish Poetry, Collections, Lp3.

Scouring, Um9.

Scranton, Pennsylvania, U. S. Hu9.

Screw Cutting, Ue2.

Screw Propulsion, Ue4.

Scripture, History, T3.

Scriptures, T2.

Scrofula, Disease, M3.

Scroll Sawing, Fa6.

Scrotum, Disease, Mg9.

Sculptors' Lives, B.

Sculpture, Fd7.

Scurvey, Disease, M3.

Sea, Adventures, V7.

Sea, Bathing, Mh4.

Sea, Mosses, Nh6.

Sea, Physical Geography, Ng9.

Sea, Power, Cn.

Sea Shore, Nh6.

Sea, Zoology, Nh6.

Seal, Animal, Nh6.

Seals, Fe3.

Seamanship, Cn5.

Seamen's Lives, B.

Seashore, Nh6.

Seasickness, M3.

Seasons, Na9.

Seaweed, Nh6.

Sebastopol, Russia, Hr1.

Second Advent, T5.

Second Adventists, Tc7.

Second Sight, Ep9.

Secondary Batteries, Pe2.

Secondary Schools, E1.

Secret Service, S3.

Secret Societies, H9.

Secret Writing, Eb2.

Sects, Christian, Tc.

Securities, Se8.

Sedition Law, Jt.

Seedlings, Farming, Af.

Seedlings, Gardening, Ag.

Seeds, Farming, Af.

Seeds, Gardening, Ag.

Seismology, Ng8.

Self-Culture, E5.

Selkirk, History, Hb5.
Seminaries, T1.
Seminole Indians, Hu1.
Semitic Language, Ek9.
Senegal, History, Ho6.
Senegambia, Ho5.
Sensation, Ep4.
Sense, Ep2.
Sepoy War, History, Hc5.
Sepulchres, Ag9.
Sepulture, Hygiene, Mh9.
Serbia, History, Hg6.
Serfdom, Russian History, Hr.
Serfdom, Slavery, S6.
Sermons, T7.
Serpent Worship, Tn7.
Serpents, Nh6.
Servants, D.
Servia, History, Hg6.
Servian Language, Ek9.
Service Books, T8.
Settlements, S9.
Seven Weeks' War, Hg.
Seven Years' War, Hg.
Seventh Day Adventists, Tc7.
Sewage, Analysis, Ue8.
Sewage, Hygiene, Mh1.
Sewerage, Engineering, Ue8.
Sewerage, Sanitary, Ub8.
Sewing, Dc.
Sewing Schools, S9.
Sex, Ethics, Ep6.
Sex, Evolution, Mb.
Sex, Manners and Customs, H8.
Sextant, Na5.
Sexual Science, Disease, Mg9.
Sexual Science, General Mg5.
Sexual Science, Special Mg6.
Shade Drawing, Fd3.
Shadow Pantomimes, Fs4.
Shadows, Drawing, Fd3.
Shafting, Ue1.
Shakers, Tc8.

Shakespeare, Bacon Controversy, Ls4.
Shakespeare, Biography, Ls3.
Shakespeare, Criticism, Ls2.
Shakespeare, Theatres, Ls9.
Shakespeare, Works, Collective, Ls.
Shakespeare, Works, Separate Plays, Ls1.
Shanghai, History, Hc.
Sharks, Nh6.
Shawnee Indians, History, Hu1.
Sheep, A4.
Sheet Metal Works, Um1.
Sheffield, England, Hb1.
Shell, Guns, Cn1.
Shell, Mounds, N.
Shells, Zoology, Nh6.
Shells and Shell Guns, Cn1.
Sheriffs, Sg8.
Shingles, Disease, M3.
Ship Building, Cs.
Ship Building, Naval Architecture, Cn9.
Ship Fever, M3.
Shipping, C1.
Ships, History of, Cs1.
Shipwrecks, V7.
Shoemaking, Ut6.
Shoes, Clothing, Dc.
Shooting, Fs9.
Shooting Stars, Na2.
Shops and Foundry, Ue2.
Shore, Nh6.
Shorthand, Eb2.
Showcard Writing, Fd9.
Shows, Amusement, Fs2.
Shrimp, Nh6.
Shrines, T9.
Shrubbery, Ag6.
Shrubs, Nh2.
Siam, History, Hc4.
Siam, Voyages and Travels, Vc4.

Siberia, History, Hr2.

Sicily, History, Hi2.

Sick, M3.

Sieges, Cm1.

Sierra Leone, History, Ho5.

Sight, Me2.

Sign Language, Ek1.

Sign Painting, Ub6.

Signals, Block, Ue7.

Signals, Electric, Pe5.

Signals, Military, Cm1.

Signals, Navigation, Cm5.

Signals, Railway, Ue7.

Signals, Telegraph, Pe8.

Signatures, Ep7.

Signboards, Eb.

Signboards, Painting, Ub6.

Signets, Fe3.

Sikkim, History, Hc5.

Silesia, History, Hc1.

Silhouettes, Fd1.

Silk, Manufactures, Um8.

Silk Worm, A8.

Silos, A4.

Silver, Coinage, Se7.

Silver, Metallurgy, Ue9.

Silver, Mineralogy, Ng6.

Silver, Money, Fe5.

Silver, Plating, Pe2.

Silversmithing, Fe8.

Sin, T6.

Sinai, History, Hc9.

Sinai, Voyages and Travels, Vc9.

Sindh, History, Hc5.

Singapore, History, Hc5.

Singers' Lives, Fm9.

Singing, Instruction Books, Fm2.

Singing, Vocal Music, Fm3.

Singing, Voice, Culture, Fm7.

Sinus, Disease, M5.

Sioux Indians, Hu1.

Sisterhoods, Catholic, Tc2.

Sisterhoods, Protestant Episcopal, Tc3.

Six Nations, Indians, Ha2.

Skating, Fs8.

Skeleton, Animal, Nh.

Skeleton, Human, Ma.

Skepticism, Tn6.

Sketching, Fd1.

Skin, M4.

Skull, Ma1.

Sky, Na.

Slander, Ethics, Ep4.

Slander,Law, Jp.

Slang, Ek4.

Slave Trade, S6.

Slavery, S6.

Slavonia, History, Hg3.

Slavonic Language, Ek9.

Sleep, Ethics, Ep9.

Sleep, Hygiene, Mh5.

Sleep, Walking, Ep9.

Sleight of Hand, Fs5.

Slide Rule, Pm5.

Slide Valve, Ue5.

Sloyd, E3.

Smallpox, M3.

Smell, Ethics, Ep2.

Smell, Physiology, Ma2.

Smelting, Ue9.

Smoke, Chimneys, Ub9.

Smoke, Hygiene, Mh1.

Smoking, M7.

Smoking, Ethics, Ep4.

Smuggling, Jt.

Smyrna, History, Hc7.

Snakes, Nh6.

Snow, Ng7.

Soap, Manufactures, Um7.

Sobriquets, G2.

Social Science, S.

Social Settlements, S9.

Socialism, Se5.

Societies, Architecture, Fs7.

Societies, Art, F7.
Societies, Charitable, S9.
Societies, Educational, E9.
Societies, Secret, H9.
Society, E7.
Society Islands, History, Hc2.
Society of Jesus, Tc2.
Socinianism, Tn5.
Sociology, S.
Sodium, Pc5.
Sofia, History, Hg4.
Sogdiana, History, Hc5.
Soil Draining, Af1.
Soils, Af1.
Solar System, Na.
Soldering, Ub8.
Soldiers' Lives, B.
Solids, Geometry, Pm4.
Solids, Physics, Pc.
Solitaire, Cards, Fs3.
Solitude, Ep2.
Solomon, Song of, Bible, T2.
Solomon Islands, History, Hc3.
Solution, Chemical, Pc.
Solution, Electrical, Pe2.
Solution, Mathematical, Pm6.
Somaliland, History, Ho4.
Somerset, England, Hb1.
Somme, History, Hf1.
Somnambulism, Ep9.
Sonatas, Score, Fm4.
Sonatas, Vocal, Fm3.
Song of the Children, Bible, T2.
Songs, Fm5.
Sonnets, Lp.
Sonora, History, Ha5.
Sorcery, Ep9.
Sore Throat, Me5.
Sorghum, Af6.
Soubriquets, G2.
Soudan, History, Ho3.
Soul, Ethics, Ep2.
Sound, P4.

South Africa, History, Ho7.
South African Republic, Ho7.
South America, History, Ha8.
South America, Voyages and Travels, Va8.
South Australia, History, Hc3.
South Carolina, U. S. Hu9.
South Dakota, U. S. Hu9.
South Pole, Vn2.
South Sea Islands, History, Hc2.
Sovereigns' Lives, B.
Space, Astronomy, Na.
Space, Metaphysics, Ep2.
Spain, History, Hs.
Spain, Army and Navy, Hs3.
Spain, Separate Places, Hs1.
Spain, Voyages and Travels, Vs.
Spanish Drama, Lp5.
Spanish Language, Ek7.
Spanish Literature, L5.
Sparring, Fs1.
Sparta, History, Hk5.
Speakers, Lr.
Speaking, Lo.
Specie, Se7.
Species, Origin of, Mb.
Specific Gravity, Pc4.
Specifications, Building, Ub.
Spectacles, Eye, Me2.
Spectacles, Optics, P2.
Spectres, Ep9.
Spectroscope, P2.
Spectrum Analysis, Pc2.
Speculation, Banks, Se8.
Speculation, Ethics, Ep5.
Speech, Ek3.
Speech, Organs of, Ma2.
Speeches, Collections, Lo6.
Speeches, Individual, Lo5.
Spelling Books, English, Ek2.
Spherical Geometry, Pm4.
Spherical Trigonometry, Pm6.
Spices, Af6.

Spiders, Nh4.

Spine, M5.

Spinning, Um8.

Spirals, Geometry, Pm4.

Spires, Fa2.

Spirit, T5.

Spiritism, Ep9.

Spirits, Ep9.

Spiritualism, Ep9.

Spirituous Liquors, Manufacture, Db.

Spirituous Liquors, Temperance, M7.

Spite, Ethics, Ep4.

Spitzberger, Vn.

Spleen, Disease, M3.

Spoils System, Sg.

Sports, General, Fs.

Sports, Indoor, Fs2-5.

Sports, Outdoor, Fs6-9.

Spring, Nh.

Springfield, Illinois, U. S. Hu9.

Springfield, Massachusetts, U. S. Hu9.

Springfield, New Jersey, U. S. Hu9.

Springfield, Ohio, U. S. Hu9.

Springs, Ng9.

Stables, A6.

Staffordshire, England, Hb1.

Stage, Lp1.

Stage, Ethics, Ep5.

Stage Coaches, Ut1.

Stained Glass, Fc2.

Staining, Ub6.

Stair Building, Ub4.

Stammering, M5.

Stamps, Postage, Fe6.

Standards, Flags, Be9.

Starch, Um5.

Star Fish, Nh6.

Stars, Na1.

Starvation, Mf9.

State and Church, Tc.

State, Ethics, Ep5.

State, Political Science, Sp.

State Rights, Jn.

Staten Island, New York, U. S. Hu9.

Statesmanship, Sp.

Statesmen's Lives, B.

Statics, P3.

Stationery, Um3.

Statistics, Business, Eb.

Statistics, Mathematics, Pm9.

Statistics, Public, S2.

Statuary, Fd7.

Statutes, Law, J.

Stavonia, History, Hg3.

Steam, Ue5.

Steam Boilers, Ue5.

Steam Engine, Ue5.

Steam Fitting, Ub9.

Steam Heating, Ub9.

Steam Navigation, C1.

Steamboats, Construction, Cs5.

Steamships, Construction, Cs5.

Steel, Bridges, Ue6.

Steel, Engraving, Fe3.

Steel, Foundry, Ue2.

Steel, Manufacture, Um1.

Steel, Metallurgy, Ue9.

Steel, Square, Ue.

Steel, Structures, Ub.

Steeples, Fa2.

Stella Astronomy, Na1.

Stenography, Eb5.

Stereography, Pm4.

Stereometer, P4.

Stereopticon, P2.

Stereoscope, P2.

Stereotomy, Pm.

Stereotyping, Fd8.

Stills, Db.

Stimulants and Narcotics, M7

Stimulants and Narcotics, Ethics,
Ep4.
Stock Breeding, A4.
Stock Companies, Se8.
Stock Exchange, Se8.
Stockings, Clothings, Dc.
Stockings, Manufacture, Um8.
Stocks, Se8.
Stoics, Philosophy, Ep1.
Stomach, Mf2.
Stone, Ub1.
Stone Age, N.
Stone Cutting, Ub1.
Storage Batteries, Pe2.
Stories, Authorship, Lb1.
Storms, Ng7.
Story Telling, Lo.
Stoves, Um1.
Strains, Building Materials, Ue6.
Strasburg, History, Hf6.
Strategy, Cm1.
Strawberries, Ag3.
Street Cleaning, Ue8.
Street Railroads, Ue7.
Streets, Ue6.
Strength of Materials, Ue6.
Stress of Materials, Ue6.
Strikes and Lockouts, Se4.
Stucco, Ub2.
Stuttering, M5.
Style, Costume, Dc3.
Style, Manners and Customs, H8.
Styria, History, Hg3.
Subconsciousness, Ethics, Ep2.
Subconsciousness, Sleep, Ep9.
Submarine Building, Cn9.
Submarine Warfare, Cn1.
Subways, Ue7.
Success, E5.
Suffering, Ethics, Ep9.
Suffering, Physical, M.
Suffrage, Sp.
Suffrage, Woman, S8.

Sugar, Chemistry, Pc9.
Sugar, Cane, Af6.
Sugar, Manufacture, Um5.
Suggestion, Mental, Ep9.
Suicide, M6.
Suicide, Ethics, Ep5.
Suits at Law, Jt.
Sulphur, Pc5.
Sumatra, History, Hc3.
Summer, Nh.
Sun, Na1.
Sun Dials, Na9.
Sunday, T8.
Sunday Schools, Tc9.
Sunlight, Mh1.
Sunstroke, M3.
Supernatural, Ep9.
Superstition, Ep9.
Supply and Demand, Se4.
Suppuration, Ms.
Sureties, Js.
Surgeons' Lives, B.
Surgery, Ms.
Surgical Instruments, Ms6.
Surnames, Bc8.
Surrogate, Law, Js.
Surrey, England, Hb1.
Surveying, Pm6.
Surveying, Astronomy, Na8.
Susanna, Story of, Bible, T2.
Susiana, History, Hc6.
Sussex, England, Hb1.
Swallows, Nh7.
Swaziland, History, Hc7.
Swearing, Ethics, Ep5.
Swearing, Law, Jp.
Sweden, Army and Navy, Hd8.
Sweden, History, Hd6.
Sweden, Separate Places, Hd7.
Sweden, Voyages and Travels, Vd.
Swedenborgianism, Tc7.
Swedish Architecture, Fa.
Swedish Drama, Lp9.

Temperaments, Ep4.
Temperance, Ethics, Ep4.
Temperance, Hygiene, M7.
Temperate Clime, Products of, Af2.
Temperate of Body, M3.
Tempering, Metal, Um1.
Templars, Knights, H9.
Temples, Fa2.
Temporal Power, Tc2.
Temptation, Ethics, Ep4.
Temptation, Sin, T6.
Ten Commandments, T2.
Ten Tribes of Israel, Hc8.
Tenant, Law, Jp.
Tenant, Political Economy, Se3.
Tenement Houses, Fa4.
Tennessee, U. S. Hu9.
Tennis, Fs8.
Tents and Tenting, Fs9.
Tenure of Land, Law, Jp.
Tenure of Land, Political Economy, Se2.
Terminology, Ep2.
Terra cotta, Architecture, Fa.
Terra cotta, Building Material, Ub1.
Terra cotta, Manufacture, Um4.
Testimony, Jt.
Testing Materials, Ue6.
Tetanus, M3.
Texas, U. S. Hu9.
Text Books, E3.
Textile Fabrics, Manufactures, Um8.
Thanksgiving Day, H8.
Theatre, Lp1.
Theatre, Architecture, Fa3.
Theatre, Fakes, Fs2.
Theatricals, Private, Lp4.
Theatricals, Public, Lp.
Thebes, History, He.
Theft, Law, Jt.

Theism, Tc1.
Theodicy, T5.
Theological, Education, T.
Theological Schools, T.
Theology, Devotional, T9.
Theology, Doctrinal, T4.
Theology, General Works, T.
Theology, Natural, Tc1.
Theology, Practical, T9.
Theosophy, Tn1.
Therapeutics, M3.
Thermodynamics, Pe.
Thermometer, P3.
Thessalonians, Bible, T2.
Thieves, Jt.
Thinking, Ep3.
Thirty-nine Articles, Tc3.
Thirty Years' War, History, Hg.
Thorough Bass, Fm1.
Thought, Ethics, Ep3.
Thought Transference, Ep9.
Thousand Islands, New York, U. S. Hu9.
Thrift, E5.
Throat, Me5.
Thunder Storms, Ng7.
Thurlings, History, Hg1.
Thyroid Gland, Disease, M5.
Tibet, History, Hc.
Tides, Astronomy, Na4.
Tides, Physical Geography, Ng9.
Tierra del Fuego, History, Ha8.
Tigers, Nh3.
Tiles, Building, Ub1.
Tiles, Manufacture, Um4.
Timber, Material, Ub.
Timber, Trees, Af9.
Timbuctoo, History, Ho5.
Time, Chronology, Na9.
Time, Philosophy, Ep2.
Timekeepers, Ut3.
Timothy, Bible, T2.
Tin, Manufacture, Um1.

Tin, Metallurgy, Ue9.
Tin, Roofing, Ub5.
Tissues, Animal, Nh3.
Tissues, Human, Ma.
Tithes, Jp.
Titus, Bible, T2.
Tlingit Indians, Ha3.
Toads, Nh6.
Toadstools, Ag.
Toasts, Lq.
Tobacco, Culture, Af2.
Tobacco, Ethics, Ep4.
Tobacco, Hygiene, M7.
Tobit, Bible, T2.
Tobogganing, Fs8.
Toilet, Domestic Economy, Dc8.
Toilet, Hygiene, Mh3.
Tokio, History, Hc1.
Toleration, Ep5.
Toltec Indians, Ha5.
Tombs, Ag9.
Tombstones, Fd7.
Tools, Building, Ub3.
Tools, Machine, Ue3.
Tools, Printing, Fd8.
Toothache, Ms7.
Topographical Drawing, Fd3.
Topography, Maps, Fd3.
Topography, Surveying, Pm6.
Tories, American, Sp3.
Tories, English, Sp4.
Tornadoes, Ng7.
Torpedoes, Manufacture, Pc9.
Torpedoes, Naval Science, Cn1.
Tortoise, Nh6.
Torts, Jp.
Torture, Inquisition, Tc.
Torture, Law, Ja.
Total Abstinence, Ep4.
Total Depravity, T6.
Touch, Ep2.
Toulouse, History, Hf1.
Touraine, History, Hf1.

Tournaments, H8.
Towers, Architecture, Fa.
Town Planning, Sg4.
Towns, Sg.
Toxicology, M7.
Toys, Fs.
Toys, Electrical, Pe9.
Trachea, Disease, M3.
Tracheotomy, Ms.
Tract Societies, Tc9.
Tractarianism, Tc3.
Traction Engines, Ue5.
Tracts, General, Tc.
Tracts, See Special Religion.
Trade, Law, Jn.
Trade Mark, Patents, U3.
Trade Marks, U3.
Trade Unions, Se1.
Trades, Ut.
Traditions, Ep9.
Tragedy, Lp.
Training, Fs1.
Trains, Ue7.
Tramps, S4.
Tramways, Ue7.
Transcendentalism, Ep2.
Transcriptions, Music, Fm4.
Transformers, Pe2.
Transit, C2.
Transits, Na.
Transmigration, Ep2.
Transmutation of Metals, Pc1.
Transportation, C2.
Transubstantiation, T8.
Transvaal, History, Ho7.
Transylvania, History, Hg3.
Trapping, Fs9.
Trappists, Roman Catholic Order, Tc2.
Travancore, History, Hc5.
Traverse Tables, Pm6.
Travelers' Lives, B.
Travels, General, V8.

Travels, Tales of, V9.
Treason, Jt.
Treaties, Jn.
Trebizond, History, Hc7.
Trees, Botany, Nh2.
Trees, Forestry, Af9.
Trees, Ornamental, Ag6.
Trenton, New Jersey, U. S. Hu9.
Trespass, Jp.
Trials, Jt.
Triangles, Geometry, Pm4.
Triangles, Trigonometry, Pm6.
Tricks with Cards, Fs5.
Tricycling, Fs8.
Triest, History, Hg3.
Trigonometry, Pm6.
Trinidad, History Ha6.
Trinity, T5.
Trinity, Knights of, H9.
Tripoli, History, Ho3.
Triumphal Arches, Fd7.
Tropical Products, Af6.
Trotting, Fs8.
Troubadours, Lp5.
Trouveres, Lp5.
Troy, Ancient, History, Hc7.
Troy, New York, U. S. Hu9.
Trumpet, Fm8.
Trunks, Ut9.
Trusses, Building, Ue6.

Trusses, Surgical, Ms6.
Trusts, Sel.
Truth, Ep4.
Tsimsheans Indians, Ha2.
Tuberculosis, Me5.
Tudors, English, Hb.
Tudors, Irish, Hb2.
Tumors, M3.
Tuning Fork, P4.
Tuning Fork, Music, Fm8.
Tuning Pianos, Fm8.
Tunis, History, Ho3.
Tunnels, Ue9.
Turbines, Ue8.
Turin, History, Hil.
Turkestan, History, Hc5.
Turkey, History, Ho.
Turkey, Voyages and Travels, Vo.
Turkey, in Asia, History, Hc7.
Turkish Language, Ek9.
Turkish Literature, L8.
Turning, Lathe Work, Ue2.
Tuscany, History, Hil.
Twins, Mg2.
Type, Fd8.
Typewriter, Eb6.
Typhoid Fever, M3.
Typhus Fever, M3.
Typography, Fd8.
Tyrol, History, Hg4.

—U—

Uganda, History, Ho5.
Ukraine, History, Hr2.
Ulcers, Ms.
Ultramontanism, Tc1.
Umbrella, Ut9.
Umbria, Hil.
Unbelief, Tn6.
Understanding, Ep3.
Union City, New Jersey, U. S. Hu9.

Unions, Sel.
Unitarianism, Tc6.
United Brethren, Tc6.
United Presbyterians, Tc5.
United States Army and Navy, Hu3.
United States, Civil War, Hu6.
United States, Colonial, History, Hu2.
United States, Constitution, Sp3.

United States, Descriptive, Hu.

United States, General History, Hu3.

United States, Government, Sp3.

United States, Military Academy, Cm.

United States, Naval Academy, Cm.

United States, Navy, Hu3.

United States, Periods, 1775-1800 Hu4.

United States, Periods, 1801-1859, Hu5.

United States, Periods, 1860-1865, Hu6.

United States, Periods, 1866-1900, Hu7.

United States, Periods, 1901-, Hu8.

United States, Revolution, Hu4.

United States, Separate States, Cities and Towns, Hu9.

United States, Voyages and Travels, Vu.

United States, War with Germany, Hu8.

United States, War with Spain, Hu7.

United States of Columbia, Ha8.

Units, Pm5.

Unity, Ethics, Ep2.

Universal, History, H4.

Universalism, Tc6.

Universe, Astronomy, Na.

Universe, Geology, Ng.

Universities, El.

University Extension, El.

University Settlement, S9.

Upholstery, Art, Fa6.

Upholstery, Domestic Economy, D9.

Upper Austria, History, Hg3.

Uranium, Pc5.

Urine, Chemistry, Pc7.

Urns, Metal, Um1.

Urns, Pottery, Fc.

Uruguay, History, Ha8.

Usages, E7.

Useful Arts, U.

Usury, Js.

Utah, U. S. Hu9.

Utilitarianism, Ep6.

Utopia, Sp.

Utrecht, Treaty, H3.

—V—

Vacations, H8.

Vaccination, M3.

Vacuum Tubes, Radio, Wireless, Pe8.

Vagabonds, S4.

Vagrancy, S4.

Valdenses, Tc6.

Valencia, History, Sp1.

Valleys, Ng8.

Value of Money, Pm9.

Valves, Steam, Ue5.

Valves, Water, Ue8.

Vancouver's Island, History, Ha2.

Van Dieman's Land, History, Hc3.

Vapor, Ng7.

Vapor Engines, Ue5.

Variation of the Compass, Cn5.

Variola, M3.

Varioloid, M3.

Varnish, Chemistry, Pc9.

Varnishing, Ub6.

Vases, Metal, Um1.

Vases, Pottery, Pc.

V—Continued.

Vassals, Sp.
Vatican, Tc2.
Vatican, Council, Tc2.
Vaudois, Tc6.
Vaults, Architectural, Fd3.
Vaults, Engineering, Ue6.
Veda, Tn1.
Vegetables, Ag1.
Vegetarianism, Mf1.
Vehicles, Automobile, Ut5.
Vehicles, Carriages, Ut1.
Vehicles, Chariots, H8.
Vehicles, Wagons, Ut1.
Veins, Ma1.
Velocipedes, Fs8.
Vendors, Law, Jp.
Venereal Diseases, Mg9.
Venesection, M3.
Venezuela, History, Ha8.
Venice, History, Hi1.
Venice, Voyages and Travels, Vi.
Ventilation, Ub9.
Ventriloquism, Fs5.
Venus, Na2.
Vera Cruz, History, Ha5.
Vermont, U. S. Hu9.
Verona, History, Hi1.
Versailles, History, Hf1.
Versification, Ek4.
Vertebrates, Paleontology, Ng3.
Vertebrates, Zoology, Nh3.
Vespers, T8.
Vespers, Music, Fm5.
Vessels, Cs.
Vestments, T8.
Veterinary, Science, A6.
Viaducts, Ue6.
Vice, Law, Jc.
Vice, Social Science, S3.
Victoria, History, He3.
Victorian Literature, L4.
Vienna, History, Hg3.
Vikings, Hd3.

Village Communities, Sg.
Villages, Sg.
Vilas, Fa4.
Vine, Grape, Ag3.
Vinegar, Db1.
Vines, Botany, Nh1.
Vines, Gardening, Ag.
Violin, Fm8.
Violincello, Fm8.
Virgin Islands, History, Ha6.
Virgin Mary, T5.
Virginia, U. S. Hu9.
Virtue, Ep5.
Viscera, Ma.
Vision, Ethics, Ep2.
Vision, Eye, Me2.
Vision, Optics, P2.
Visions, Ep9.
Vital Statistics, S2.
Vivisection, Nh3.
Vocal Culture, Fm7.
Vocal Elocution, Mp1.
Vocal Music, Fm3.
Vocal Organs, Disease, Me5.
Vocal Organs, Physics, P1.
Vocal Organs, Singing, Fm7.
Vocalists' Lives, B.
Vocational Education, E4.
Vocational Psychology, Ep2.
Voice, Elocution, Lo.
Voice, Physical Culture, Mp1.
Voice, Physiology, Me5.
Voice, Singing, Fm7.
Volapuk, Ek9.
Volcanoes, Ng8.
Voltaic Cell, Pe2.
Voltaic Electricity, Pe4.
Volumetric Chemistry, Pc3.
Volumetric Geometry, Pm4.
Voodooism, Ep9.
Voting, Sp.
Voyages, Arctic, Vn.
Voyages, Discovery, V4.

200

Voyages, Round World, V3.
Voyages, Stories of, V9.

Voyages and Travels, V.
Vulgarism, Ek4.

—W—

Wager of Battle, Jt.
Wagers, Ep4.
Wages, Se4.
Wagons, Ut1.
Waihu Island, History, Hc2.
Waikna Indians, Ha5.
Waldeck, History, Hg1.
Waldenses, Tc6.
Wales, History, Hb4.
Wales, Separate Cities, Towns, Etc., Hb5.
Wales, Voyages and Travels, Vb5.
Walking, Sports, Fs1.
Walks, Garden, Ag6.
Wallachia, History, Hg4.
Wall Paper, Designing, Fd4.
Wall Paper, Hanging, Uc7.
Wall Paper, Manufacture, Um3.
Walls, Construction, Ub1.
Walls, Engineering, Ue6.
Waltz, Dancing, Fs4.
Waltz, Ethics, Ep4.
Waltz, Music, Fm4.
Wampanoag Indians, Hu1.
War, H8.
War, Ethics, Ep5.
War of 1914-1920, General History, Gp3. See also under Countries engaged.
War of 1914-1920, Political Economy, Under Nations, Sp.
War of the Roses, Hb.
War Poetry, Lp2.
Wards, Js.
Warming, Nb9.
Warnings, Ep9.
Warsaw, History, Hr1.

Warwick, England, Hb.
Washing, D1.
Washington, D. C., U. S. Hu9.
Wasps, Nh4.
Watches, Ut3.
Water, Chemistry, Pc3.
Water, Engineering, Ue8.
Water, Hygiene, Mh1.
Water, Meteorology, Ng7.
Water Color Painting, Fd1.
Water Cure, M9.
Water Power, Ue8.
Water Supply, Ue8.
Water Wheels, Engineering, Ue8.
Water Wheels, Hydraulic, P6.
Waterfalls, Ng9.
Waterloo, Batle, Hf.
Waterspouts, Ng9.
Waterworks, Ue8.
Waves, Electric, Pe8.
Waves, Hydraulics, P8.
Waves, Physics, P2.
Wax, Um7.
Wax Flowers, Dc7.
Wealth, Se.
Weapons, Arms, Cm1.
Weapons, Manners and Customs, H8.
Weather, Ng7.
Weaving, Um8.
Weddings, Manners and Customs, H8.
Weeds, Nh1.
Weights and Measures, Pm5.
Welding, Um1.
Wells, Ue8.
Wer-Wolves, Ep9.

Wesleyans, Tc4.

West Indies, Ha6.

West Indies, Voyages and Travels, Va6.

West Point, New York, U. S. Hu9.

West Point, Military Academy, Cm.

West Virginia, U. S. Hu9.

Western Africa, History, Ha6.

Western Australia, History, Hc3.

Western Islands, History, Hs7.

Westmoreland, England, Hb1.

Westphalia, History, Hg1.

Whale, Nh8.

Whale, Fishing, V5.

Wheat, Af2.

Wheeling, Fs8.

Wheels, Ut1.

Whigs, England, Sp4.

Whigs, United States, Sp3.

Whipping, Corporal Punishment, E3.

Whipping, Law, Jt.

Whirlwinds, Ng7.

Whist, Fs3.

Whooping Cough, Disease, M3.

Widows, S7.

Wife, S7.

Wight, Isle of, History, Hc1.

Wigs, Manufacture, Um3.

Wigs, Toilet, Dc8.

Will, Ethics, Ep2.

Willow Work, D8.

Wills, Js.

Wind, Ng7.

Windmills, Ue3.

Window Dressing, Eb8.

Window Gardening, Ag5.

Windows, Architecture, Fa.

Windows, Stained Glass, Fc2.

Winds, Ng7.

Windward Islands, History, Ha6.

Wine, Manufacture, Db1.

Wine, Temperance, M7.

Wings, Nh7.

Winter, Nh.

Wire, Um1.

Wiring, Pe7.

Wireless Telegraphy, Pe8.

Wisconsin, U. S. Hu9.

Wisdom, Bible, T2.

Wit and Humor, Lw.

Witchcraft, Ep9.

Witnesses, Jt.

Wives, S7.

Woman, S7.

Woman Suffrage, S8.

Women, Diseases of, Mg.

Women, Employment, S8.

Wonders of the World, G7.

Wood, Carving, Fe3.

Wood, Engraving, Fe.

Wood, Material, Ub.

Wood, Polishing, Ub6.

Wood, Trees, Af9.

Woodcraft, Fs9.

Woodcuts, Fe1.

Woodwork, Ub4.

Wool, Dyeing, Um9.

Wool, Manufactures, Um8.

Worcester, England, Hb1.

Worcester, Massachusetts, U. S. Hu9.

Words, Ek3.

Work, Se4.

Workhouses, S4.

Working Classes, Se4.

World, Geography, V1.

World, Voyages Around, V3.

World's Fair, U.

Worms, Nh4.

Worry, Ethics, Ep3.

Worship, T8.

Worsteds, Dyeing, Um9.

Worsteds, Manufacture, Um8.

Wounds, Ms.

Wrecks, V7.
Wrestling, Fs1.
Writers' Lives, B.
Writing, Ek2.

Wrongs, Jp.
Wurtemburg, History, Hg1.
Wyoming, U. S. Hu9.

—X—

X-Ray, Pe6.

Xylography, Fe.

—Y—

Yacht Building, Cs4.
Yacht Racing, Fs6.
Yachting, Fs6.
Yarn, Dyeing, Um9.
Yarn, Manufacture, Um8.
Year Books, Gr1.
Yeast, Pc9.
Yellow Fever, M3.
Yellowstone Park, U. S. Hu9.
Yemen, History, Hc7.
Yezo Islands, History, Hc1.
Yoga, Tn4.
Yonkers, New York, U. S. Hu9.

York, Pennsylvania, U. S. Hu9.
Yorkshire, England, Hb1.
Yorktown, Virginia, U. S. Hu9.
Yorktown, Virginia, Revolution-
ary War, U. S. Hu4.
Yosemite Valley, U. S. Hu9.
Young Men, Ep5.
Young People, Ep5.
Young Women, Ep5.
Yucatan, History, Ha5.
Yugoslavia, History, Hg4.
Yukon, History, Ha3.

—Z—

Zambesi, History, Hc7.
Zanzibar, History, Ho5.
Zechariah, Bible, T2.
Zend Avesta, Tn4.
Zephaniah, Bible, T2.
Zinc, Ue9.
Zinc Oxide, Pe9.
Zither, Fm8.
Zodiac, Na.

Zodiacal Light, Na.
Zoological Gardens, Nh3.
Zoological Mythology, Nh9.
Zoology, Nh3.
Zoophytes, Nh6.
Zoroaster, Religion, Tn4.
Zululand, History, Ha7.
Zurich, History, Hf8.

Lightning Source UK Ltd.
Milton Keynes UK
UKHW011001100720
366326UK00003B/877